Praise for *Appropriate*

"A very fine, subversively original new play . . . 'I ended up deciding I would steal something from every play that I liked,' Jacobs-Jenkins says, 'and put those things in a play and cook the pot to see what happens.' What a difference a chef makes. Mr. Jacobs-Jenkins, who is in his late twenties, honors the time-tested recipes of those who have gone before him, combining them into a crafty narrative guaranteed to hook susceptible theatergoers. But he also brings a culinary self-consciousness to the mix that makes you savor the ingredients anew, while pondering why they have dominated American theater for so long . . . The style of *Appropriate* is piercingly clear, with carefully drawn characters who speak in crisp and fluid dialogue . . . It also turns out that *Appropriate* is, at heart, a ghost story, in the most profound sense. The play begins in sustained darkness, as we listen to a harried, scraping musical noise that seems both eerie and utterly natural. It's the sound of cicadas, we later learn, making the calls they do every so many years just before dying. They can't help themselves. Without forcing us, this remarkable and devious play allows us to draw our own parallels with the human sound and fury that fills most of the evening."
— BEN BRANTLEY, *NEW YORK TIMES*

"*Appropriate* feels entirely original and upsetting in new ways . . . It asks audiences to understand the hatred, the anger and the pathologies that evolved as a result of our racist past. Eventually the [family's] house buckles under the weight of those emotions, underscoring the metaphor. The effect is visceral, reverberating for days afterward."
— JOANNE OSTROW, *DENVER POST*

"*Appropriate* is a highly charged and ambitiously sprawling drama . . . The author finds opportunities to startle us just as we're settling back to enjoy the familiar spectacle of flamboyant family dysfunction . . . There's no denying that Jacobs-Jenkins is one of the rising stars in the American theater."
— CHARLES McNULTY, *LA TIMES*

Praise for *An Octoroon*

"From Dion Boucicault's 1859 play *The Octoroon*, about a white Southerner who falls in love with a mixed-race woman, Jacobs-Jenkins fashioned a kind of theater-essay, whose parentheses are filled with dialogue about performing blackness, the theater as a live art, and the basic concerns that haunt the thinking mind trapped in a body that's defined by skin color, gender, or speech: life makes each of us a target for someone else. *An Octoroon* isn't just an alternative to the irony-free 'black American theater' of Lorraine Hansberry and August Wilson; it's part of it—and part of many other things, too, because Jacobs-Jenkins's surrealism grows out of naturalism, the strange circumstances that make us open our mouths, hoping to be heard, even as we forget to listen. By experimenting with numerous theatrical genres in a single work, like *An Octoroon*, Jacobs-Jenkins is displaying how serious he is about the form. Again and again, he poses these questions: What can the theater do, besides talk? What makes a play? Is it love?"

—HILTON ALS, *NEW YORKER*

"A coruscating comedy of resolved history . . . Strange as it seems, a work based on a terminally dated play from more than 150 years ago may turn out to be this decade's most eloquent theatrical statement on race in America today."

—BEN BRANTLEY, *NEW YORK TIMES*

"*An Octoroon* is a meta-dramatic meditation and deconstructive masterpiece . . . Jacobs-Jenkins writes brilliantly about race in America, and the cultural legacy employed in the service of tyranny since the earliest days of this nation. He knows how to curse through stereotypes and rip apart the fault lines of representation . . . Jacobs-Jenkins stands out because his writing lets you into the pain of his own process. His explorations feel like they flow in real time and only have been wrought at considerable personal cost to a writer. A writer who cannot help but wonder aloud if anyone profiting from such a history, however critical he or she might be, could be said to be anything other than complicit . . . There is no smugness or surety to what we watch: *An Octoroon* constantly worries about sensationalism and exploitation and, especially, what it is asking actors to do. Jacobs-Jenkins knows he is asking his collaborators to trust him through their own discomfort and go to places few care to visit."

— CHRIS JONES, *CHICAGO TRIBUNE*

"If I say that this bizarrely brilliant play is the work of a thirty-two-year-old black American dramatist called Branden Jacobs-Jenkins, I am already subscribing to an idea the piece seeks to subvert: that our identities can be defined by convenient labels. Even the notion of what makes a 'play' is up for grabs, as this tumultuous piece is both an adaptation of *The Octoroon*, a popular nineteenth-century melodrama by Dion Boucicault, and a postmodernist critique of it . . . A work that is infinitely playful and deeply serious and which dazzlingly questions the nature of theatrical illusion . . . An extraordinary play that defies categorization and that proclaims Jacobs-Jenkins as an exciting new dramatist who questions what it means to be dubbed 'a black playwright.'"

— MICHAEL BILLINGTON, *GUARDIAN*

APPROPRIATE / AN OCTOROON

APPROPRIATE / AN OCTOROON

Plays

BRANDEN JACOBS-JENKINS

THEATRE COMMUNICATIONS GROUP
NEW YORK
2019

Appropriate/An Octoroon: Plays is published by Theatre Communications
Group, Inc., 520 Eighth Avenue, 24th Floor, New York, NY 10018-4156

The publication of *Appropriate/An Octoroon: Plays* by Branden Jacobs-
Jenkins, through TCG's Book Program, is made possible in part by the
New York State Council on the Arts with the support of Governor Andrew
Cuomo and the New York State Legislature.

Special thanks to the Vilcek Foundation for its generous support of this
publication.

TCG books are exclusively distributed to the book trade by Consortium
Book Sales and Distribution.

Library of Congress Cataloging-in-Publication Data
Library of Congress Control Numbers:
2018013232 (print) / 2018017625 (ebook)
ISBN 978-1-55936-490-4 (trade paper) / ISBN 978-1-55936-801-8 (ebook)
A catalog record for this book is available from the Library of Congress.

Book design and composition by Lisa Govan
Cover design by Monet Cogbill
Cover lithograph: "A Cotton Plantation on the Mississippi," 1884,
Currier & Ives; Library of Congress

First Edition, March 2019
Third Printing, March 2022

CONTENTS

APPROPRIATE

Production History

Appropriate received a co–world premiere at the 37th Humana Festival of New American Plays at the Actors Theatre of Louisville (Les Waters, Artistic Director; Jennifer Bielstein, Managing Director) in Louisville, KY, on March 5, 2013, in association with Victory Gardens Theater. It was directed by Gary Griffin. The scenic design was by Antje Ellermann, the costume design was by Connie Furr-Soloman, the lighting design was by Matt Frey, the sound design was by Bray Poor; the dramaturgs were Janice Paran and Amy Wegener, and the production stage manager was Michael D. Domue. The cast was:

TONI	Jordan Baker
RHYS	David Rosenblatt
BO	Larry Bull
RACHAEL	Amy Lynn Stewart
CASSIDY	Lilli Stein
AINSLEY	Gabe Weible
FRANZ	Reese Madigan
TRISHA	Natalie Kuhn

Appropriate received a co–world premiere at the Victory Gardens Theater (Chay Yew, Artistic Director; Christopher Mannelli, Managing Director) in Chicago, IL, on November 14, 2013. It was produced in association with the Actors Theatre of Louisville and the 37th Humana Festival of New American Plays. It was directed by Gary Griffin. The scenic design was by Yu Shibagaki, the costume design was by Janice Pytel, the lighting design was by Jesse Klug, the sound design was by Chris LaPorte, the prop design was by Jesse Gaffney; the fight choreographer was Ryan Bourque, and the stage manager was Dennis J. Conners. The cast was:

TONI	Kirsten Fitzgerald
RHYS	Alex Stage
BO	Keith Kupferer
RACHAEL	Cheryl Graeff
CASSIDY	Jennifer Baker
AINSLEY	Theo Moss, Mark Page
FRANZ	Stef Tovar
TRISHA	Leah Karpel

Appropriate was produced by Woolly Mammoth Theatre Company (Howard Shalwitz, Artistic Director; Jeffrey Herrmann, Managing Director) in Washington, DC, on November 8, 2013. It was directed by Liesl Tommy. The scenic design was by Clint Ramos, the costume design was by Kathleen Geldard, the lighting design was by Colin K. Bills, the original music and sound design were by Broken Chord; the fight choreographer was Joe Isenberg, the production dramaturg was Kirsten Bowen, and the production stage manager was Kristy Matero. The cast was:

TONI	Deborah Hazlett
RHYS	Josh Adams
BO	David Bishins
RACHAEL	Beth Hylton
CASSIDY	Maya Brettell
AINSLEY	Cole Edelstein, Eli Schulman
FRANZ	Tim Getman
RIVER	Caitlin McColl

Appropriate received its New York premiere at Signature Theatre (James Houghton, Founding Artistic Director; Erika Mallin, Executive Director) in New York on February 25, 2014. It was directed by Liesl Tommy. The scenic and costume design were by Clint Ramos, the lighting design was by Lap Chi Chu, the original music and sound design were by Broken Chord, the fight direction was by Rick Sordelet and Christian Kelly-Sordelet, the projection design was by Aaron Rhyne; the production stage manager was Kyle Gates. The cast was:

TONI	Johanna Day
RHYS	Mike Faist
BO	Michael Laurence
RACHAEL	Maddie Corman
CASSIDY	Izzy Hanson-Johnston
AINSLEY	Alex Dreier
FRANZ	Patch Darragh
RIVER	Sonya Harum

Appropriate was produced at Center Theatre Group's Mark Taper Forum (Michael Ritchie, Artistic Director; Stephen D. Rountree, Managing Director) in Los Angeles, CA, on September 23, 2015. It was directed by Eric Ting. The scenic design was by Mimi Lien, the costume design was by Laura Bauer, the lighting design was by Christopher Kuhl, the sound design was by Matt Tierney; the fight director was Steve Rankin, the dramaturg was Joy Meads, and the production stage manager was David S. Franklin. The cast was:

TONI	Melora Hardin
RHYS	Will Tranfo
BO	David Bishins
RACHAEL	Missy Yager
CASSIDY	Grace Kaufman
AINSLEY	Liam Blair Askew, Alexander James Rodriguez
FRANZ	Robert Beitzel
RIVER	Zarah Mahler

Dramatis Personae

ANTOINETTE "TONI" LAFAYETTE	the oldest, white, late 40s–early 50s
RHYS THURSTON	her son, white, late teens
BEAUREGARDE "BO" LAFAYETTE	the middle, white, late 40s–early 50s
RACHAEL KRAMER-LAFAYETTE	his wife, white, late 40s
CASSIDY "CASSIE" KRAMER-LAFAYETTE	their oldest child, white, early teens
AINSLEY KRAMER-LAFAYETTE	their youngest child, white, a child
FRANÇOIS "FRANZ/FRANK" LAFAYETTE	the youngest, white, late 30s–early 40s
RIVER RAYNER	his fiancée, white, early 20s but looks younger

Setting

The living room of a former plantation home in southeast Arkansas. Summer.

A Note on Overlapping

A slash (/) in a character's line denotes where the following character's line should begin.

A slash (/) at the beginning of a line denotes a complete overlap with the following character's line.

A Note on the Title

ap pro pri ate

adj.   1. suitable or fitting for a particular purpose, person, occasion, etc.

      2. belonging to or peculiar to a person; proper

v.   3. to set apart, authorize, or legislate for some specific purpose or use

      4. to take to or for oneself; take possession of

      5. to take without permission or consent; seize; expropriate

      6. to steal, especially to commit petty theft

LOPAKHIN: If only my father and grandfather could rise up out of their graves, and see all that's happened—how their little Yermolai, their abused, semi-literate Yermolai, who used to run around barefoot in winter—how that same Yermolai has bought this estate, the most beautiful spot on earth. Yes, I've bought the land on which my father and grandfather were slaves, where they weren't even allowed in the kitchen.

—ANTON CHEKHOV, *THE CHERRY ORCHARD*

No "we" should be taken for granted when the subject is looking at other people's pain.

—SUSAN SONTAG, *REGARDING THE PAIN OF OTHERS*

ACT ONE

The Book of Revelations

PROLOGUE

Light abandons us and a darkness replaces it.

Instantly, a billion cicadas begin trilling in the dense, velvety void—loudly, insistently, without pause—before hopefully, at some point, becoming the void.

The insect song fills and sweeps the theater in pulsing pitch-black waves, over and beyond the stage—washing itself over the walls and the floors, baptizing the aisles and the seats, forcing itself into every inch of space, every nook, every pocket, hiding place and pore until this incessant chatter is touching you.

It is touching you.

This goes on and on and on and on and on until the same thought occurs in every head:

"Is this it?"

"Is this the whole show?"

1

Then moonlight happens.

It seeps in through an upstage window and just barely reveals a large and very disorderly living room in an old plantation home somewhere in Arkansas.

A mixture of old and new furniture is scattered beneath a dead chandelier; a wall or two is lined with semi-stuffed bookshelves; others are spotted with the memories of old photographs and dusty generic oil paintings. A staircase disappears into another floor, a swinging door opens onto a dining area/kitchen, and a hallway leads to an unseen room or two, probably connected to the dining area. Through a foyer, a front door with transom windows leads out onto a porch.

As the light swells, the cicadas fade to a place just beyond us but never disappear.

Somewhere, an adult-sized figure is curled up on a couch, a quilt pulled up over its head. The figure is moving slightly: the rise and fall of its breathing.

After a moment, a man with a backpack suddenly springs up into a window far from the front door—Franz. He holds a phone flashlight in his hand. Balancing on something, he jostles with the frame for a bit before hoisting it up. As someone unseen hands him another backpack and some camping equipment—which he tosses into the house—her sleepy-sounding voice is heard.

RIVER: What is that?

FRANZ: What is what?

RIVER: That sound.

FRANZ: Cicadas.

RIVER: What?

FRANZ: They're bugs. Every thirteen years they come out of the ground and make all this noise together. I forgot all about them.

(Franz climbs through the window and, with his phone's light, immediately starts taking the place in.)

RIVER: It's so beautiful . . .

FRANZ: Uh, okay . . . If you're not careful, they'll get caught in your hair, so stay away from the trees. That's where they all gather.

(Beat, as Franz tries to find a light switch before he is distracted by a scraping noise from outside.

Suddenly, someone—River—shoots up into the window and tries to pull herself in, sort of in slow motion, but she doesn't quite make it, falling back down. River tries to spring up into the window, again, and, again, she doesn't make it. Eventually, Franz notices.)

Baby, what is happening?

RIVER: I'm too sleepy! Help! *(Gets help)* How long were we on the road?

FRANZ: Twenty hours—watch your he—?

RIVER *(Hits her head hard)*: OW!!!

FRANZ *(Putting her in)*: I said, watch your head.

RIVER *(Rubbing her head)*: Owwwww-wuh!

FRANZ *(Holding her, rubbing her head)*: Aww, come here. *(Kissing her head, eating her "booboo")* Nom-nom-nom.

(Beat, as River takes a look around.)

RIVER: . . . This is it?

FRANZ: Yeah . . . what?

RIVER: I didn't saying anything! . . . It's just different from what I imagined.

FRANZ: Which was what?

RIVER: I don't know—when you said plantation, I thought more . . . *Gone with the Wind*, less . . . hoarding. But I love it?

FRANZ: We were supposed to turn it into a Bed and Breakfast.

RIVER: What happened?

FRANZ: Jesus, River, you just said it—my father was a fucking / hoarder!—

RIVER: Hey hey hey—stop it. Stop. No anger. Let it go. *(Beat, looking around)* So you grew up around all this?

FRANZ: Someone's actually cleaned up a bit—if you'll believe it. *(Fidgeting)* Though I don't know how they think they're going to get rid of this place with it looking like this.

RIVER *(Noticing, calming his fidget)*: You're nervous.

FRANZ: Yeah.

RIVER: Well, don't be because you've got me here. And, if you ever get nervous, just look for me—besides, you have a right to be here. This is your house, too. They can't do anything with it without you. Plus you grew up here. You lived with him. And you deserve what you're asking for. You deserve it. Say "I deserve it."

FRANZ: I deserve it.

RIVER: Good. *(Kisses him before a creak is heard)* What was that?

(Beat.)

FRANZ: . . . It's my dad.

RIVER: Stop!

FRANZ: I'm joking—it's an old house—

RIVER: Spirits are not a joke! You know I'm sensitive!

FRANZ: Please. You just went clomping through that cemetery with no problem.

RIVER: What cemetery?

FRANZ *(Gesturing out a window)*: On the way up here. What did you think that was—all those stones? That little gate?

RIVER *(Looking out the window)*: That's not a—I thought it was like a cute little patio—stop! / Stop messing with me.

FRANZ *(Looking out the window)*: I guess it sort of looks like a—what? It's true! The tombstones are just knocked over. See? Five generations of us are out there. That's how long this place has been in the family.

(Beat, before River hits him.)

Ow! River!

RIVER: Why did you let me do that? *(Gasp, realizing)* I forgot my sage!—

FRANZ: Will you stop it—

RIVER: Stop what? Spirits are real and our bodies are just porous vessels of energy vulnerable and susceptible to corruption and influence and— *(Off Franz's reaction)* Don't look at me like that! I don't know if I can sleep here—

FRANZ: River, I was just messing with you. It's an old cemetery and an old house that creaks. There are no spirits here. Trust me. I would know. You and that stupid shaman.

RIVER: My shaman is not stupid. The world is a very old place full of all kinds of things . . . *(Beat)* Your father's not out there, is he?

FRANZ: No. I think they buried him back in DC next to Mom . . .

RIVER: Who knocked over the tombstones?

FRANZ: Probably kids from the town.

(Beat.)

Or maybe me when I was drunk. I don't remember.

RIVER *(Referring to the cemetery)*: Why didn't you tell me about this?

FRANZ: I forgot. *(Pointing out the window)* But you see that lake there?

RIVER: Yeah . . . ?

FRANZ: Well, through those woods alongside it is where all the slaves were buried, but you have to go looking for that. They don't have grave markers or anything . . .

RIVER: Oh no . . .

(Beat.)

FRANZ: BAHHH!!!

RIVER *(Shrieks a little, then)*: STOP! / YOU JERK!

FRANZ: / WOOOOOAAAHHHAAAHAAHAAAAA!

RIVER: STOP, FRANZ! I SAID / STOP—!

(Suddenly, the quilted figure on the couch springs up with a moan, freaking River and Franz out.)

FRANZ: AHHHH / —OOOOHHH—WAHHHHHH!

RIVER: AAAAHHHH—EEEEEE—IIIIIIIII!

(Franz and River cling to each other. After a moment, the figure removes the quilt. It's Rhys, half asleep. Beat, as he and Franz recognize each other through the gloom.)

FRANZ: Rhys? Is that you?

RHYS: Uncle Frank?

FRANZ *(Relieved)*: Oh man! Yeah, man! I almost just killed you! Holy—I haven't seen you since you were . . . you look . . . like a dude, dude! What are you doing here?

RHYS *(Guarded, a little confused)*: I'm here with Mom.

FRANZ: I thought you guys weren't coming in until tomorrow?

RHYS: Mom fired the estate people, so we had to come down early to get everything ready ourselves . . . What are you doing here?

FRANZ: I'm here for the auction. *(Beat)* Why are you sleeping down here? Aren't there beds upstairs?

RHYS: Aunt Rachael needs the other bedrooms for her and Bo and their kids and they get in / today—

FRANZ: Oh, right . . .

RHYS *(Sees River)*: Does Mom know you were coming?

FRANZ: I guess not, ha ha. *(Following his gaze)* Oh, sorry, this is—

RIVER: Hi, I'm—I'm Aunt River, I guess— / Eek!

FRANZ: You're not Aunt / Anybody. Quit it!—

RIVER: You are / so cute—

(River is interrupted by a beam of light seen scurrying down the walls at the top of the stairs, followed by Toni in her sleeping gown. She is frightened and pissed off and wielding a large flashlight, which she shines in everyone's faces.)

TONI: What in God's name—

(Light on Rhys.)

Rhys? What—

(Light on River, gasping, hysterical.)

WHO THE HELL ARE YOU?!

(Stunned, River shields her eyes and moves closer to Franz, who catches the glare of the beam.)

FRANZ: Toni——

TONI: Frank!? What in fuck's sake is going on? What are you doing here?

FRANZ: Will you turn that thing off?

TONI: How did you get in here? / What are you doing here?

FRANZ: We came in through the window! Turn that off!

TONI *(Crosses to window to secure it)*: Through the / window!?

FRANZ: Calm down. You weren't supposed to be here yet!

TONI: Don't tell me to calm down! I thought you were looters! And how do you know when I'm supposed to be here? And who in God's name is this?

(Beat.)

FRANZ: It's nice to see you, too.

TONI: Oh shut up Frank. You shut the hell up. It is not nice to see you right now. Where have you been for the last . . . Did you know our father is dead?!

FRANZ: Yeah and no one told me——

TONI: No one told——how was anyone supposed to tell you anything when no one knows where you've been for the last umpteen years——ten years?! There are lawyers trying to find you, Frank! Where have you even been?! What is going on? And what exactly are you doing here now? What are you doing?

(Beat.)

FRANZ: I have to talk to Bo.

(Beat, in which Toni seems to bristle.)

TONI: Talk to Bo about what?!

FRANZ: I have something I need to say to him.

TONI: Well, Bo's not here——

FRANZ: I know that——

TONI (*Referring to River*): Who is this?!

FRANZ: This is River.

RIVER: Hi, Toni.

(*Beat.*)

TONI: Frank, are you high?

FRANZ: Nobody is high—

TONI: Then are you out of your mind? Do you know what is happening here? This is not some sort of crash pad / party house—

FRANZ: Toni, we just drove twenty hours to get here and now that we're here, we're going to bed—

TONI: Whoa, Frank, whoa. No!

FRANZ: This is my house, too, you know! / And I have a right to be here—

RIVER: / Franz—

TONI: Actually, Frank, it's nobody's house now!

FRANZ: Well, until tomorrow, I still own a third of this house, which means I own a third of the bedrooms, which means I can do whatever the hell I want with them!

(*Beat.*)

TONI: You don't own a third of the rooms, dummy. You own a third of each room—and Rachael already reserved the other bedrooms and how do you know what is / happening tomorrow?

FRANZ: River, grab your bag—

TONI: No, Frank, no! I will call the cops.

FRANZ: Then call the cops!

(*Toni and Franz stand off a beat before Franz exits up the stairs. River follows.*)

RHYS: What the fuck was that?

TONI: Shh, Rhys!

RHYS: Are you going to call the cops?

TONI: No.

RHYS: Why not?

TONI: He's right. They wouldn't do anything. The place is still
his. This is unbelievable. My heart is racing. You don't just
show up like this—did he seem high to you?

RHYS: No.

TONI: How old did that girl look?

RHYS: I don't know. Twenty something? What do we do?

TONI: I don't know. I don't know. Bo will be here soon. Thank
God. He'll know what to do.

(Beat.)

Wait—why are you down here?

RHYS: The attic is full of mosquitoes.

TONI: Do you want to just come upstairs and sleep with me in
Grandpa's room?

(Beat.)

RHYS: No.

(Beat.)

TONI: Well I'm not getting back to sleep now. I might as well
get up and start working on all this. Why don't you go up
there by yourself and rest? You can take the bed. *(Beat)*
Go on. Otherwise, I'll just keep you up. *(Beat, before Rhys
gets up)* Hey—I don't know what Frank is doing here, but
you stay away from him, okay? We're going to let your
Uncle Bo handle it.

RHYS: Okay.

TONI: He is not going to ruin our time here together. This
weekend is about us.

RHYS: Sure.

(*Rhys starts to exit.*)

TONI: Can I have a hug before you go?
RHYS: Uh, sure.
TONI: I love you. Every morning I wake up, I thank God for you.
RHYS: Love you, too.

(*Rhys exits upstairs. Toni is alone. She looks around a bit, tries to shake off what's just happened. She takes a deep breath or something.*)

TONI: Oh, Daddy . . .

(*Blackout, in which the cicadas' twittering swells and swells and swells and swells before hitting a peak and dissolving back into a hum.*)

2

The same living room, later that morning.

It being brighter, the house's true state is revealed: a little claustrophobic. All over, there is junk—just a ton of it—a whole lifetime of clutter and crap everywhere it can possibly be.

Tables are in the process of being set up around the space, some already burdened with various secondhand knickknacks, clothing, and soft goods, to which Toni attends, while talking.

Newly arrived Rachael stands near the door to the kitchen, partially eavesdropping on something.

TONI: Then I asked him why he was here, he said, "I have to talk to Bo." So I thought, okay, let him talk to Bo.

RACHAEL: About what?

TONI: Who knows? He wouldn't tell me. But can you believe he had the nerve to stand there, shouting at me about no

one telling him Daddy was dead? You know we tried to
find him—

RACHAEL: Yes—and where is he now?

TONI: Upstairs sleeping.

RACHAEL: Where?

TONI: His old room.

(Beat.)

RACHAEL: But I reserved that room for the kids.

TONI: I told him but he just shoved right past me.

*(A hyperactive Ainsley comes tearing through the room,
making a toy fly. He beelines for the swinging door, but
Rachael cuts him off.)*

RACHAEL: Heyhey—not in there! And no running. It's too hot.
(To Toni) And who is this in the kitchen?

TONI: His entourage? No idea. But at least she looks legal, right?

RACHAEL: And what is she doing?

TONI: Well, she just came down stairs a couple of hours ago
and just started making breakfast apparently—

RACHAEL: / What?

TONI: I have never heard of a stranger walking into a dead
man's house and just helping themselves to the kitchen.

RACHAEL *(To Toni)*: And you didn't say anything to her?

TONI: What was I going to say? "Don't do that"? I don't know
who this girl is. She could be hopped up on meth for all
I know—

RACHAEL: Oh my God, Toni, what?

TONI: Or—I mean, I don't know—

RACHAEL: She's not high, is she? Is she actually high?

TONI: No. I don't think so. I mean, they didn't seem high last
night. I threatened to call the police like I used to and they
didn't flinch so I just assumed. Honestly, if you ask me,
all he's doing is sniffing around for money, which is just

disgusting. You don't know about your father's funeral, but you know the exact date his house gets auctioned off? I call bullshit.

RACHAEL: Toni—sorry—your language—?

TONI: Sorry—

RACHAEL: It's okay. Ainsley's just picking up all sorts of / things—

TONI *(A look toward the swinging door)*: Bo sure is taking his time with her . . .

(Beat.)

RACHAEL *(Seeing Toni work)*: Toni, let me help you—

TONI: No, no, Rachael. I'm just . . . separating things into piles.

RACHAEL: Okay and the auction is still happening tomorrow, right?

TONI: For the house yes, but, for the rest of this stuff, I thought, "Why don't we just have a little estate sale instead?" I figured it would save us some time—

RACHAEL: Okay and—I'm sorry, Bo didn't really tell me the whole story—these liquidator people quit?

TONI: No, no. I fired them. They were robbing us blind.

(Suddenly, Bo enters from the kitchen, looking a little over-extended, iPhone in hand. Beat.)

BO: So that's River.

RACHAEL: River?

BO: Yes, as in the body of water, and she's a part-time chef at a vegan restaurant in Portland, Oregon, and she's making us all breakfast—

TONI: / What?

RACHAEL: Why?

BO: Because she wants to be helpful—

TONI: Why?

BO: Because she's Frank's fiancée—

TONI: What?

BO *(Overwhelmed)*: I'm sorry, Franz. He's calling himself Franz now for some goddamn reason—Jesus Christ, I need to sit for a second—

TONI: How old is she?

BO: Was I supposed to ask her that?

RACHAEL: Is she high?

BO: / I don't know . . .

TONI: What does he have to talk to you about?

BO: I have no idea. She said it was not hers to tell. Jesus, is there anywhere to sit down around here?

TONI: Well what do we do?

(Ainsley comes running through.)

RACHAEL *(To Ainsley)*: / Hey! What did I say? No running! Where is your sister?

(Ainsley exits.)

BO: Toni, can you give me a second please?! The flight was exhausting, I get in the door, you're raving like a lunatic—got me thinking there's a murderer in the house—

TONI: Bo, they scared the crap out of me / this morning!

BO: Well, what do you want me to do? Didn't you just say he was upstairs asleep?

TONI: Then let's go get him up! He cannot be here!

BO: Toni, no! Will you just calm the frick down? What is the use of whipping yourself into a frenzy right now? Let the man wake up first and then we'll let him say whatever he / needs to say—

TONI: And what about her—how am I supposed to get anything done with this strange girl / prancing around our kitchen?

BO: Toni! I said let the man wake up and then we'll deal with it! And, I mean, what have you even gotten done? I thought you've been here all week?

TONI: I have.

BO: Then what have you been doing? This place is a pigsty! How long has it been looking like this? I mean, what was I paying that Juanita woman for?

TONI: Juanita was a caregiver, Bo, not a housekeeper and for your information, a lot of this is stuff I had to bring down from upstairs / so that your kids could have some place to sleep!

BO: So you just spent the last week moving crap from one room to another?

RACHAEL (*Trying to calm things down*): And Toni, we are very grateful! I wasn't trying to be any sort of trouble, / on top of—

TONI: You are not being any sort of trouble, / Rachael—

RACHAEL: If I'd known that things were going to be in such a . . . state of flux, I would have found a hotel—

TONI: It's fine—

RACHAEL: I just thought it might be nice for the kids to experience some of Daddy's childhood before it disappears—

BO: This is not my *childhood*—

RACHAEL: Childhood *summers*—

BO: Barely.

RACHAEL: Ever since Ray's funeral, the kids have been nothing but questions, Toni. And I really regret now that they never . . . got to spend a lot of time with your father. Plus, Bo only ever brought me out here once and I always wanted to see this place again—one of these big, old romantic plantation homes. So I thought, since we can't do a big trip this summer, why don't the kids and I just do a little "Southern History Road Trip"? Bo has to fly back home early for work, but we rented van and the kids and I are going to start here, and drive back—through Mississippi, Louisiana—all those places—experience some of Daddy's heritage—

BO: Rachael, I grew up in DC—

RACHAEL: DC is the South.

TONI: No it isn't.

BO: She thinks anything south of Brooklyn is a trailer park—

RACHAEL: Your family is from here! Your roots are here!

TONI: You can't do a "big trip"?

BO: We can't afford it—

RACHAEL: Anyway, now that I see the job you have here, Toni, I'm glad we've all come! I'm sorry we haven't been around more to help out, but now that we're here, we're all going to make sure we pitch in and— *(To Ainsley, who runs through)* HEY! WHAT DID I SAY? STOP RUNNING BEFORE YOU CATCH A HEATSTROKE!

BO: I thought Cassidy was watching him.

RACHAEL: Like she listens to me. I don't even know where she wandered off to.

TONI: I think she went down to the lake to find Rhys. She came right in here asking after him.

BO *(To Rachael)*: What?!

RACHAEL: Stop it—

TONI: What's wrong?

RACHAEL: It's nothing, Toni. We just think Cassidy's developing a little crush.

TONI: On Rhys?

RACHAEL: Didn't you see them at the funeral? Afterwards, all Cassie could talk about was Rhys, Rhys, Rhys—went around posting these photos of the two of them together on Facebook and we were like, "Honey, please don't do that. There's a casket in the background."

BO: So let's keep an eye on the two of them, okay? I know we're in Arkansas and everything—

RACHAEL: Bo, ew! *(To Toni)* It's innocent—

TONI: Well, your little scientist is certainly sprouting into quite a pretty young thing—

RACHAEL: Those braces finally paid off.

BO: Though we're still paying off the braces—

RACHAEL: / Bo—

BO: And don't get me started on the contact lenses and the dermatologist—having a teenager in New York is a Ponzi scheme, Toni. I bet, in Atlanta, you get to have as ugly a kid as you want.

(Rhys and Cassidy enter through the front door. Rachael sees them.)

RACHAEL: Cassidy, where have you / been?!
CASSIDY: We were just checking out the cicadas—relax!
RHYS: / Are they still here?
RACHAEL: You are supposed to be watching your brother!

(Toni gives Rhys a nod.)

CASSIDY: Why?
RACHAEL: Because I said so! Now take him please?
CASSIDY: Take him where?
RACHAEL: Toni, can we put these kids to work?
CASSIDY: / Oh my God.
TONI: Actually, you guys wanna finish cleaning out Grandpa's study? I already started.
RACHAEL: That's perfect.
TONI *(Hands Rhys some empty boxes)*: Just put anything that looks like we can sell it in these and throw everything else away, okay?
RHYS: Okay.
RACHAEL: And take your brother!—
CASSIDY: Ugh!

(Rhys, Cassidy and Ainsley exit upstairs.)

BO: Rhys is looking good.
RACHAEL: Yes, so healthy.
TONI *(Sheepishly, making a joke)*: Well, at least he's not in jail, right?

(Beat.)

RACHAEL: Have you guys figured out what you're going to do in the fall?

TONI: Not really. Technically, he has to get his GED now, so he's taking a year off. Also wants to spend some more time with his father, he says . . .

BO: What does that mean?

(Bo's phone dings and he deals with it.)

TONI: I guess he's moving out of my house and into Derek's . . . But, you know what I was thinking? What if me and Rhys came up to New York for a visit with you guys this fall? Or maybe even just Rhys? Maybe he could stay a week or two with you all? A month?

(Beat, no response.)

But there's no pressure. I'm just sick of only seeing each other under such dark circumstances.

(Ainsley runs right back down the stairs.)

RACHAEL *(To Ainsley)*: THAT'S ENOUGH! COME HERE! SIT DOWN! SIT DOWN!

(Rachael grabs a photo album off the shelf.)

/ HERE! LET'S LOOK AT SOME PICTURES OR SOMETHING. DISTRACT YOURSELF.

TONI: Are you going to stay on that phone all weekend?

BO *(Looking up from his phone)*: Don't start with me. You know, no wonder those estate people wanted more money. I would have given it to them if I'd known it was this bad.

TONI: They were crooks, Bo—

BO: Well how about next time you let me be the judge of that since I'm the one actually taking the hits?

TONI: Taking what "hits"?!

BO: Toni, who has been bankrolling our father's convalescence the past two years—

TONI: What!?

BO: Who's been keeping these lights on? Who was footing the bill for this so-called "caretaker," that took / care of what exactly?

TONI: Wait, I'm sorry—so you're looking for a return on your *investment*? / Our father was dying!

BO: I'm saying this has been a very expensive journey, Toni, and I think I deserve not to have the little that I'm entitled to jeopardized by your shortsightedness / again and again—

TONI: And what about my *time*, Bo? Do you think I'm going to get back every twelve-hour drive I had to make to deal with doctors, / and arrangements for the funeral—

BO: / Oh, here we go—

TONI: —so you and Rachael couldn't miss whatever dinner party you / needed to be at?

BO: No one told you to do all that stuff by yourself. If you needed help, you could have asked for it, which you didn't do, / which you never do, because you're a control freak!

TONI: Oh, I'm sorry! I didn't know I was supposed to be *applying* for your assistance!

BO: I'm sorry I thought you were competent enough to do / what you said you could do!

TONI: I'm sorry some of us's time isn't more important / than everyone else's!

BO: I'm sorry some of us don't have fat alimony checks to fall back on!

(Beat.)

TONI: I wasn't aware that my divorce was such a luxury—

BO: That is not what I—look, Toni. Everyone knows that you have had—have been having a very, very difficult year, years—but I feel that it has been irresponsible and unfair of you to hold the rest of us . . . hostage to your . . . hardship. Our father just died. You have been going through a divorce. There was Rhys's whole . . . ordeal. You were obviously in no position to accept the responsibility of executor and you should have had the . . . self-awareness to say something.

(Beat.)

TONI: Well. Fuuuuuuuuuuuuuuuuuuuuuuuuuuuuuuuuuuuuuuuck you!

RACHAEL: Toni, your / language!

TONI: Rachael, why don't you take your kid somewhere else?! Because we're having an adult conversation in here!

(Beat, as Rachael gives Bo a look and maybe takes Ainsley into another room or maybe just crosses to stand closer to him, wherever he is. In any case, she plants herself somewhere where she can still keep an ear on the fight.)

BO: Toni, look at what you just spent all week doing—

TONI: You know, despite my recent trials, Bo, I am not suddenly some sort of moron. Now I'm sure that, had you been named the executor, you and your personal assistant Sonya would have done an effortlessly more wonderful job and come tomorrow we'd all be wiping our behinds with hundred dollars bills but, unfortunately, that is not—for whatever reason—how Daddy saw to it. Now if you have a problem with that, you can take it up with him but, in the meantime, you'll have to excuse me for not milking this very emotionally distressing experience for every penny like some kind of shylock. I'm sorry that, in the wake of our father's dying and the loss of this family's entire legacy, I can't be focused on lining your pockets but I have a feeling that whatever remainder we split after the

sale tomorrow morning and after this big old house is auctioned off will be just enough to cover your "expenses"?
But if that's not enough for you, you can just take my
share, okay? Since I'm apparently swimming in alimony.
Is that what you wanted to hear, you greedy sack of crap?

BO: Sale? What sale?

TONI: We're having an estate sale—

BO: What?! When?!

TONI: Before the auction. The estate people didn't finish cataloging everything for the auction, so I just thought why
don't we just sell it all? I already ran it by / the lawyers—

BO: Toni, that was the point of your coming down here! You
were supposed to finish cataloging everything!

TONI: Well, I ran out of time—

BO: So we're going to give everything away?!

TONI: We're not giving anything away! It's a sale!

BO: Toni, you do not make actual money off—we are not going
to pay off half a million dollars from a junk sale!

TONI: The house is going to cover the payoff, Bo!

BO: You actually think we're going to—oh my God! This is an
actual disaster!

TONI (*Off Bo's reaction*): Okay, you know what, Bo, how about
this!? How about you take over then, since I'm so goddamn
stupid! How about that!? By the powers vested in whatever, you, Beauregarde "Big Daddy" Lafayette, are now
the flipping executor! Please take over!

(*River, in an apron, pokes her head in through the swinging
door, interrupting.*)

RIVER: Quinoaffles are ready! Come and get 'em!

(*Everyone looks at her.*)

BO: Thank you.

(River exits. Bo walks away from Toni.)

TONI: That's it, Bo. Just walk away. Walk away.

RACHAEL *(To Ainsley)*: / Hey, monster, let's go get your sister.

BO: You do know this house is worthless, right?

TONI: What?

BO: Well, while you were sitting around being a nightmare, I consulted a friend of mine—an actual estate lawyer— and turns out the only people interested in land this size are retail developers, so the minute anything is signed, this house is getting demolished—

TONI: Okay—

BO: But none of that even matters, because we've also got a graveyard outside stinking up the property value!

TONI: What?

RACHAEL *(To Ainsley)*: / I said, let's go—

BO: Toni, do you have any idea how expensive it is to dig up a graveyard? You think anyone's gonna wanna be bothered with all the historical ordinance crap it'll take to turn this place into a Walmart or whatever-the-hell? We're sitting on a hard sell! We were actually counting on the proceeds from this auction to make the payoff! And we don't get anything unless we make / the payoff!

RACHAEL: / What are you— Oh my God.

TONI: Oh, so one of your New York friends swoops in and decides / everyone else is incompetent!?

RACHAEL: / Oh my God!

BO: Okay, you know what? The answer is no. I don't want to be executor. I want you to know that the responsibility is yours / when there is literally nothing left tomorrow—

RACHAEL *(Snatching the photo album away)*: Give me that! Go—go upstairs to your sister / —go!

(Ainsley runs off to the dining room.)

BO *(Distracted, to Rachael)*: Rachael? What's going on?

(Rachael, not hearing Bo, opens the photo album and stares. Her eyes scan the page for a beat, slowly, taking it all in, repulsed.)

TONI: Rachael, what's wrong?
BO: Honey?

(Standing there, Rachael flips to the next page, just as Toni and Bo rush over to see what she's looking at.)

RACHAEL *(Overwhelmed)*: Oh my God.

(Blackout. Cicadas.)

3

The living room, a bit later.
Franz sits somewhere, the album open on his lap. Bo and
Toni, standing or perched nearby, study him closely. Rachael
sits some distance away, trying to get a hold of herself. Franz
looks through the photos for a beat, before:

BO: Toni thought they might have been yours.
FRANZ: What would I be doing with something like this!?
TONI: Isn't half this crap yours? And you're the one with the
track record for freaky stuff—
FRANZ: OH MY GOD!
BO: Hey! Hey! All right! So they don't belong to Frank!—
FRANZ: No.
BO: And you've never see them before?
FRANZ: No, never.

BO: Great. Then can we hurry up and get rid of these things? It's bad enough my kid's been exposed to this bullshit once.

FRANZ: Cassidy found these?

BO: No, my other kid.

(Beat.)

FRANZ: You have another kid?

(Bo and Toni share a look.)

BO: I have an eight-year-old son, Frank. His name is Ainsley.

(Beat.)

TONI *(Wryly)*: Welcome back. Now who's your kid? *(Beat, off his reaction)* That coed in our kitchen—Brook—River— Seabreeze?

FRANZ: Oh my God—

TONI: And why is she calling herself that?! And why is she calling you *Franz*?

FRANZ: Because that's my name!

TONI: No, Frank! Your name is Frank!

RACHAEL: HELLO!?!? *(Beat)* Can we sit around being casually dysfunctional later and focus for one second?

BO: / Rach—

RACHAEL: *What* are we going to do with these photos? I mean, what in the world was your father even thinking having them out in the open like this?

TONI: Rachael, we are just as upset as you are, but let's not get irrational. We have no idea where these came from.

RACHAEL: Frank just said they weren't his, Toni, and he's the only other person who lived in this house—

TONI: They could have been here when he and Daddy moved in—there was all kinds of stuff in the attic—

RACHAEL: We didn't find these in any attic. They were sitting on the shelf right here with all of your father's things!

BO: Rach—

RACHAEL: Bo, you've got one more time to try and shush me!

TONI: And there were all kinds of people coming through here—

RACHAEL: Okay, so you want me to believe that some "friend" of your father came over and was just like, "Doop-de-doop, let me just leave my disturbing photographs of dead black people I carry around with me all the time on this shelf over here while I pay old Ray a visit" and completely forgot about them? *(Beat)* These belonged to your father. And let me just say I resent you standing there and calling me irrational. Your child was not exposed to this . . . sickness. A small child!

(Beat.)

TONI: Well, what would you like us to do, Rachael?

RACHAEL: Excuse me?

TONI: Tell me what you would like the adults in this room to do right now to help you deal with that? I mean, you handed these things over to Ainsley yourself.

RACHAEL: Oh, okay, so whatever psychological damage my child has just incurred due to his grandfather's . . . *prejudice* is now *my* fault?

TONI: *Prejudice?*

RACHAEL *(A breath, then)*: Listen, Toni: I appreciated Ray just as much as anyone and, yes, he cannot be held responsible for how he may have been brought up to feel or think about other people—

TONI: What?

RACHAEL: Toni, none of us are strangers to the history of the South. We're all standing in the middle of your family's plantation for / crying out loud!

TONI: Our father spent half of his life in Washington!

RACHAEL: But he came back here, didn't he? This is the soil upon which / his worldview was fashioned—

TONI: Rachael, you didn't even know this man!

RACHAEL: Toni, he was the grandfather of my children. I am not some / stranger.

TONI: Being a *daughter-in-law* does not make you privy to the full understanding of a person, my dear.

RACHAEL: And neither does being a daughter. My dear. Your father was a somebody long before you came along. And certainly somebody else when you weren't in the room. Now, I'm not saying Ray took these photos. I'm not saying he was involved in any of these lynchings . . . I don't know and frankly I don't care. I am just saying he was a slave to his upbringing just like everyone else and, like everyone else, he had his issues. Now can we just own that and figure out what we're going to do, because there are still children in this house and I'm not interested in any more surprises!

(Beat.)

TONI: No. I want to talk about my father's "issues."

BO: Okay, you two—

RACHAEL: / Bo, shut up—

TONI: Shut up, Bo! *(To Rachael)* Go ahead.

(Beat.)

RACHAEL: Fine, Toni. You want to look at the way he treated me?

TONI: What about the way he treated you?

RACHAEL: Ray obviously had real problems with me because of my heritage and this . . . anti-Semitism was always very uncomfortable for me, and for Bo . . . So I don't think his . . . race issues are so far of / a leap to make—

41

TONI: Wait, wait, I'm sorry, so Rachael, let me get this straight: you think our father is a racist because you think our father is an anti-Semite because you feel like he didn't *like* you?

RACHAEL: First of all, I did not call him an anti-Semite. He was in *possession* of latent anti-Semitic traits—

TONI: Anti-Semitic traits like what?

RACHAEL: Anti-Semitic traits like wh—? Like having a problem with / Jews, Toni!

TONI: No, give me a concrete example, Rachael, of our father's "latent anti-Semitism."

(Beat.)

RACHAEL: I don't have to prove anything to you.

TONI: That's right. Because you're full of it.

(Beat.)

RACHAEL: I once overheard your father referring to me as Bo's "Jew wife." We were visiting him—here, actually!—the summer I was pregnant with Cassidy and he was on the phone and he didn't know I was standing there and I overheard him refer to me to someone as "Bo's Jew wife." "Bo and his Jew wife are here from New York." Now would someone like to explain to me why it was necessary to distinguish to whoever this person was that I was, in fact, a Jew? Why couldn't I just be Bo's wife?

TONI: Are you kidding?

RACHAEL: And that's just a small example. Your father had a very difficult time with me and the fact that I was Jewish, which is maybe why he was so distant to me and Bo and our kids—I don't know—but did I feel the need to say anything to him? No. He was an old man. You can't blame people for the ways they were raised. And do I expect you guys to totally . . . be able to grasp this? No, because you've never been discriminated against, but that's how it is.

(Beat.)

TONI: All right—Bo, I think it's time to take your wife upstairs. This is now a family-only discussion.

RACHAEL: Am I next in line for the Toni Bully Treatment? I think that must make me family!

TONI: No, Rachael. You're a Jew. And you're being kicked out because I subconsciously hate Jews and you, my dear, are a big ole Jew.

(Beat.)

RACHAEL: Well, if it's how you were raised. *(Beat)* Why don't you just call *me* a shylock?

TONI: Sure: shylock.

RACHAEL: How about a kike?

TONI: Sure: kike.

(Beat.)

RACHAEL: Excuse me—

BO: / Rach—

RACHAEL: I'm going to go check on our youngest kike.

(Rachael exits up the stairs.)

BO *(Going after her)*: Rachael! Rachael! *(Wheels around)* Toni! WHAT THE HELL WAS THAT!?

(Bo exits after Rachael.)

TONI *(Calling after Bo)*: How long was I supposed to stand there and let her insult my daddy—*our* daddy! *(Turning on Franz)* You piece of shit!

FRANZ: What?

TONI: You know our father wasn't guilty of one thing that witch just accused him of and you and Bo just sat there!

FRANZ: I thought I was going to have to break up a / fistfight!

TONI: Ungrateful! After everything that man tried to do for you—

FRANZ: Oh my God what am I even doing here?

TONI: Good question! What are you doing here, besides trying to pick a dead man's pockets!? And don't tell me to talk to Bo because / you just did—

FRANZ: I am not here to pick anyone's pockets!

TONI: Oh, really—then why are you here the day before everything gets sold off, Frank!? To "pay your respects"? The funeral was / six months ago!

FRANZ: I'm here to— / to—

TONI: To—to—to what?!

FRANZ: To apologize! Actually. I came here to apologize to you and to Bo. And I knew this might be my last chance to see you two together.

(Beat.)

TONI: That was the best you could come up with? What am I going to do with an / apology?

FRANZ: I'm a different person now, Toni!

TONI: You're not getting a dime—

FRANZ: I don't want money—I'm here to make peace!

TONI: And you've never heard of email?

FRANZ: And where was I supposed to get your email?

TONI: From whoever it was that told you we would be here— which was who exactly?

(Beat.)

FRANZ: The lawyers—they found me.

TONI: They didn't tell us. When did they find you?

FRANZ: A few weeks ago. I guess it took them so long because I . . . I changed my name and moved around a lot.

(Beat.)

TONI: To Portland.

FRANZ: And other places. I didn't even know about the funeral
until . . .

(Beat.)

TONI: And how old is this "fiancée"?

FRANZ: She is twenty-three!

TONI: Oh, she's twenty-three! She's twenty-three! You have some
nerve showing up here with a "twenty-three year old" after
how you / left—

RHYS *(From off)*: Mom?

*(Rhys and Cassidy enter from upstairs. They freeze. Cassidy
holds a box of something in her hands.)*

TONI: Rhys—

CASSIDY: Hey, Uncle Frank!

FRANZ *(A little nervous)*: / Hey, Cassidy.

RHYS *(To Toni)*: What happened?

TONI: Nothing happened. We were just talking.

RHYS: About what?

TONI: Adult stuff.

CASSIDY: We're almost adults.

TONI: Not quite. Are y'all finished upstairs?

RHYS: Almost, but we found a box of stuff in the closet we
don't know what to do with?

TONI: What kind of stuff?

*(Cassidy removes a couple of jars from the box and hands
one to Toni, as Rhys wanders over to a place near the open
photograph album.)*

CASSIDY: Old scraps of cloth and stuff, but also these jars of
like . . . weird stuff.

TONI *(Taking the jar, looking at it)*: Ew . . .

CASSIDY: Right?

TONI: Are these bones?

FRANZ *(Looks at another jar)*: This might be some sort of jerky?

CASSIDY *(Another jar)*: I think this one looks like an ear.

TONI: Cassidy! Throw these away!

CASSIDY: The whole box?

TONI: Yes!

CASSIDY: Can I keep them?

TONI: No!

CASSIDY: But they're like specimens!

TONI: They're disgusting!

RHYS *(Having noticed the open album)*: Oh shit!

TONI: / Rhys!

FRANZ *(Snatching the album away)*: Whoa.

RHYS: Sorry! What—

FRANZ: Don't touch / those.

CASSIDY: What / happened?

RHYS: What are those?!

CASSIDY: What's in that? Can I see?!

TONI: We'll explain later. Go finish upstairs, you two.

CASSIDY *(To Rhys)*: What did you see?

RHYS *(Gesturing)*: They were pictures of / like—

TONI: Rhys! What did I just say?

CASSIDY: Why can't I know?!

(Bo reenters.)

BO *(Ready for a fight)*: Toni!

CASSIDY *(Running to her father)*: Daddy!

BO: What is it, sweetie? *(Referring to the jar in her hand)* Jesus, what is / that?

CASSIDY: What are those photos?

BO *(Shooting his siblings a look, incensed)*: What!?

TONI: Rhys accidentally saw it. And then we took it away before Cassidy could.

CASSIDY: Is it naked pictures or something? I've seen porn before.

(Beat.)

BO: Excuse me!?

CASSIDY: I mean—I don't like look at it, but I've seen it. I'm almost an adult!

BO: Cassidy, enough! Do you want to lose your phone? *(Beat, takes the jar from Cassidy)* Go find your mother. She needs help with your brother.

(Beat, before Cassidy exits grumpily. Rhys stands there.)

RHYS *(To Toni)*: / What's happening?

FRANZ *(To Bo)*: She didn't see anything.

TONI: *(To Rhys)*: / Throw that stuff away and finish the study, please. I'll be up in a little bit. We'll talk.

(Bo drops the jar in the box just before Rhys exits.)

BO *(To Franz)*: I don't give a shit! Get rid of those things right now before she does and— *(Wheeling around on Toni)* Toni, Rachael actually came down here because she wanted to help you!

TONI: Implying, based on nothing, that our father was some sort of bigot—she calls that / help?

BO: So you call her a kike?

TONI: You know I didn't mean it like that!

BO: Then how did you mean it?

(Beat.)

TONI: Oh! So am I now the anti-Semite? And what's the word for her? What was that "Bo and Jew wife" moment? Our father didn't even sound like that! He was probably calling her your new wife for all we know— / she is so sensitive!

BO: Rachael's relationship to our father was *her* relationship! Okay?! Leave it alone!

TONI *(Gasp, realizing)*: Oh my God—do you actually agree with her?!

BO: I'm not getting into this with you—in fact, I don't care! Just go frickin' apologize!

TONI: I am / not *apologizing*!

BO: Fix something! You lost the house! You've screwed up the auction! Just do one thing that is actually going to help everyone!

TONI: What did our father ever do to you? What did he ever do to anyone?

BO *(Reaching for the photos)*: Frank, give me the photos—I'll toss them out—

TONI *(Snatching them away)*: No!

BO: What are you doing?

TONI *(Holding them above her head)*: You're not going to pick a fight and run away! I want you to name one thing— name one instance of our father's . . . prejudice. Either of you! Maybe he used the wrong word for somebody from time to time but that's just his generation—and it was never the—the—the N-word or anything like that! I mean, have you forgotten who our father was? Yes, he spent the last twenty years of his life rotting away in this house in this horrible town and maybe he was a little aloof at the end of his life—kept to himself—but before that he was a brilliant man—a brilliant, civilized man! Top of his Harvard Law class—not some sort of illiterate gun-toting hick! He was supposed to be a judge, for crying out loud—a Supreme Court Justice! Did he ever, ever raise us to look down on anyone or call anyone names? No! And, okay, maybe he wasn't Rachael's biggest fan. It wasn't because she was Jewish. It was because she is an *annoying person*—

FRANZ: Wait a minute.

(Beat.)

What do you mean Toni lost the house?

(Beat.)

TONI: I didn't lose the house!
FRANZ: Then what is Bo talking about? Aren't you guys selling
    the place tomorrow?
BO: Yes to pay off the bank loans?
FRANZ: What loans?
BO: Uhh the half million dollars our father took out twenty
    years ago to turn this place into the B&B that never was?
TONI: The lawyers didn't tell you any of this?
BO: Yeah, what did you think is going on here?
FRANZ: I thought you were just getting rid of the place and
    splitting the money—
TONI: Wait—I thought you weren't here for any money—

(River comes through the swinging door quietly, unnoticed.)

FRANZ *(Ignoring Toni)*: How did Toni lose it, Bo?
TONI: I did not lose it!
BO: Daddy either stopped making payments or forgot to make
    payments and Toni didn't catch it in time—
TONI: *I* didn't catch it—
BO: Toni, it was your job to keep track of his mail—

(River stands next to Franz.)

TONI: My— / What?!
RIVER *(Quietly, to Franz)*: What's happening?

(Bo and Toni stop fighting, having noticed River.)

FRANZ: Toni lost the house.

TONI: I did not lose the house and the next person I hear saying that is getting the crap beat out of them! *(To Franz)* If anyone lost the house, it's you! This debt is all yours anyway!

FRANZ: How is this my fault?

TONI: Does this place look like a Bed and frickin' Breakfast? Did any of that money go into this house? Or do you think it went into taking care of you for how many years—keeping you clothed and fed? Or did you take it, Frank? How much did you drink through? How much did you smoke through? How much did you need to run away to *Oregon*? How much went to that little girl's family? *(Turning on Bo)* And I thought *your job* was handling the finances. Why didn't *you* catch this? Why couldn't *you* talk to the bank? Oh, right—because you pawned it off on Tanya or Sonya or whoever-the-hell. *(Turning on River)* And *what* are you still doing here?!

FRANZ: Hey! Do not scream at her! *(To River)* Why are we here?! / We need to go! We should go!

RIVER: No—do it now! Now is the time!

TONI: Oh my God—actually, Frank, she's right. Since we're all here, why don't you go ahead and tell Bo what you came here to tell him? See if he can use it, because I sure as hell can't—

BO: What is going on?

TONI: He came here to "apologize"!

FRANZ: TONI!

TONI: You know what? Maybe you can take my apology and give it to Bo to give to Rachael, since she is apparently looking for one? And then when you're done, you two can go!

(Beat. Franz looks to River, who gives him an encouraging look, maybe mouths something like, "Now," and tries to fade into the background. Franz takes out a piece of paper—a

letter—and reads it to his siblings. River mouths along for part of it.)

FRANZ: So. Um. *(Reading)* "I know it's been a very long time since we've all seen each other—let alone been in the same room together—over ten years now—" *(Looking at Bo)* even longer with you, Bo— *(Reading again)* "And I know that my last few years in this house and in this town were extremely rough and I did a lot of things that I am not proud of, but I am an alcoholic. I am also a drug addict. Things you both probably knew but, worst of all, I engaged in promiscuous behavior, which embarrassed not only myself but my father as well and also you, my family. It is not a past that I am proud of, but it is one that I have been working every day of the last ten years to put behind me and I still work every day at that and today I am here to let you see that work and how hard I am trying to become a better person—a person that I know, need, and want myself to be.

Also, part of any recovery like this is about making amends, which means asking for forgiveness in addition to forgiving those who you feel have wronged you in some way.

So, in addition to showing you the new man I have become, I am also here to apologize and forgive, because if I have learned anything in the past ten years, it is how lonely life can be and I would like you all to be a part of my life again and I would very much like to be a part of yours."

(Franz finishes, perhaps puts the letter away. Beat, before Toni raises her hand.)

TONI: Pardon me—and what exactly are you "forgiving" us for?
FRANZ: I don't think that's important.
TONI: I kind of think it is, because maybe we want to apologize, too. What exactly did we do?

(Beat, in which Franz looks to River, who nods.)

FRANZ: You two left me here with a mentally ill man when I was just a kid. And I've had to live with the consequences of that my whole life.

(Beat.)

TONI *(Head in her hands)*: Lord, is this really what happens when you die? What else are we going to say about this man today? *(Beat, breath, looks up)* Okay. Well, first of all, our father was not *mentally ill—*
FRANZ: Okay—mentally unstable—
TONI: He wasn't "unstable" either—
FRANZ: Toni, you didn't live in this house with him, okay!? I think our father was bipolar. He was obviously a hoarder— not to mention severely depressed after our mother died— he had fits of mania, he was sick—but you and Bo never saw this, because you were never here! I was!

(Beat.)

TONI: Second of all, what are these *consequences* you've been living with as a result?

(Beat. Franz hesitates, again. River encourages him, again.)

FRANZ: I just believe that that experience may be why I abused certain substances, why I drank—
TONI: Okay—so it's our fault that you became a pothead and got caught with some little girl you found on the internet / and run out of town—
FRANZ: That is not—why are you / trying to embarrass me!
RIVER *(Raising her hand, beat)*: . . . Franz, it's fine. It's okay. Answer her question.

(Beat. Toni looks at River, dumbfounded.)

FRANZ *(Uncomfortable)*: I take responsibility for my actions, but I did those things in a time when I was struggling with addiction—I was not myself and I just believe that this environment had a lot to do with that—

TONI: Okay, Frank. And, finally, where was this lunatic, manic-episoding, bipolar father these last ten years Bo and I were taking care of him? Or, better yet, the ten years before that when I was taking care of both of you?

FRANZ: / What are you talking about?

TONI: You are the last person to accuse me of abandonment. Who was here checking in on you every month, cooking meals, doing your laundry, breaking up fights? Who was taking you in every holiday? Whose couch were you sulking on every Christmas, every Thanksgiving—drinking yourself into a stupor in front of my child? But this isn't about me. *(Beat)* If Daddy was depressed about anything it was you. If Daddy was crazy it was because you drove him there. This man wore himself down trying to save you. We all did. Do Bo and I have a childhood home to cry over? No, because when our mother died and you became a delinquent back in Washington, getting kicked out of every school, drinking at the tender age of thirteen, our father uprooted our entire life, our entire family, for you—to bring *you* out here—

FRANZ: To start a business—

TONI: No, to save you—

FRANZ: How was moving me out to Bumblefuck Arkansas and starting a Bed and Breakfast supposed to save me?!?

TONI: Because you were bad and it was a chance to be good, Frank!—which you couldn't be back in DC and which you were obviously just as incapable of here, because guess what? If there's a sick person in this family, it's you. Even now, can you not see what you're doing? You call this an apology? The only man we all shared is dead, we are in mourning, and after tomorrow we will be literally left with nothing—and you thought this would be the perfect time to show up out of the blue—making this all about you and your healing with your walking rape fantasy over here—

RIVER: Let's keep this about his relationship with you.

(Beat.)

TONI: Wow. *(To Franz)* So I don't buy this. There is nothing new about you. You are the same thing you've always been: a selfish person—a selfish chaotic person—a taker, who is only ever thinking about himself. I mean, how exactly was this supposed to end, Frank? You apologize and we all hug it out and tomorrow everything gets auctioned off and you'd get your third? Or what? How stupid do you think we are?

(Beat.)

RIVER: For the record, unless you can show us a will that says so, you don't have a legal right to withhold anything from him.

TONI: And what are you—a lawyer?

RIVER: My parents are.

BO: Frank . . . I accept your apology and I apologize for any wrongs you feel I've done to you—

TONI: Uh, what are you doing?

BO: I'm talking to Frank.

TONI: Are you kidding—

BO: What are you now? The forgiveness police?

TONI *(To Bo)*: I'm certainly witnessing a crime! That apology isn't yours! *You* didn't lose the hours! *I* was the one looking after him and Daddy, exposing my kid to this shit show and probably turning him into the fuckup he is now! *I* took care of our father when he ran away, while you just got to sit back and write a check from the box seats! This man might as well be a stranger to you. So guess what? That apology isn't for you to accept! That forgiveness isn't for you! It's for me! It's mine!

BO: Can you even see yourself right now? You're disgusting! You're a disgusting mess!—

TONI: I just realized: you two are the same—

BO: Have you lost your mind?

TONI: No! It was stolen from me—you all took it—the same way you took my life, my time, and I'm wasting even more of it fighting with you now—and for what?

BO: That's a great question, because, who left in this house is sympathetic to— *(Gesturing, referring to Toni)* this? Not me! Certainly not Rachael! Not Frank! Even your own son doesn't want to be around you, Toni! So ask yourself why. Ask yourself. You're like—like—like poison right now! Maybe you're the sick one!

TONI: You're right. I quit. I quit.

(Toni grabs her purse, maybe a jacket, and starts to leave.)

BO *(Exasperated, annoyed)*: Please. Please be done, Toni. Sure.

TONI: Enjoy forgiving each other! I hope you forgive each other all night long, you bunch of sorry, sorry people!

(Toni holds her keys above her head, presses a button, and there is the brief electronic tooting of her car unlocking itself outside. Beat, before she exits out the front door. Bo and Franz and River look at each other. There is the sound of Toni getting into her car, slamming the door, the car starting, the car driving away.)

FRANZ: What happened to her?

BO: What hasn't happened to her? I can't tell if she's losing her mind or if she's already lost it. *(Beat)* I shouldn't have said that thing about Rhys.

FRANZ: What happened with Rhys?

BO: He's moving in with his father.

FRANZ: Wait—Toni and Derek split up?

BO: Two years ago now. Then Rhys was busted last fall dealing drugs—pills. Some kid died, judge made an example out of Rhys, Toni lost her job—

FRANZ: Lost her job?

BO: She was vice-principal at the school. The pills were traced back to her. She was forced to resign. It was a whole mess . . .

FRANZ: She said I fucked him up? Is that my fault? Did I have something to do with that?

BO: I don't know, Frank. Did you?

(Beat.)

RIVER: Should we be worried about her?

BO: No. What's she going to do? Kill herself? She'll be back. *(Beat)* Where else does she have to go? *(Beat)* Maybe now I can actually try to figure out how to salvage this mess.

RIVER: What needs to happen?

BO: A miracle. This estate sale is a bust, the graveyard's killing the property value—

RIVER: Which one?

BO: What do you mean which one?

RIVER: Aren't there two / graveyards?—

BO: I don't even want to know! I'm hemorrhaging money just standing here! I need to find Rachael. *(Referring to the photographs, to Franz)* Will you throw those things in the garbage?

(Bo exits up the stairs. Beat.)

RIVER *(Sweetly)*: You did it!

FRANZ: She's right. This is selfish. I'm being selfish.

RIVER: That was just a step. Remember: progress, not perfection. You can't help anyone without helping yourself first.

And it sounds like Toni has demons of her own to deal with. She's so much scarier than you described.

FRANZ: She's scarier than I remember.

RIVER: It must be this house. There's so much pain here. You all just have to get this place out of your bones. Think of how good you're going to feel tomorrow, when you see it get auctioned off and become someone else's problem. You'll be free. Then you'll sleep again . . .

FRANZ: The house is already gone. The auction tomorrow is to pay off some loan Daddy had with the bank. This place was never mine.

(Beat.)

RIVER: That's fine. It's all symbolic. Don't overthink it. The universe is rooting for you. *(Referring to the album in his hands)* What is this?

FRANZ *(Embarrassed)*: Something I gotta throw away.

RIVER: What? Are they baby pictures or something? *(Wrestling it away)* Give it to me—

FRANZ: River, no!

RIVER *(Looks at it, distressed)*: Oh! *(Drops the album, having felt something)* Oh my God! *(Beat)* Franz, what was that!?

(Beat, as Franz looks at her, confused.)

FRANZ: What was what?

(Curtain. Cicadas.)

ACT TWO

Walpurgisnacht

The living room, the middle of the night.

A spray of candlelight finds River on the couch, paging through the photo album. Cassidy stands just over her shoulder, unseen, clutching her phone.

In the background, there is a barely perceptible newfound order to the place.

There is a substantial stretch of quiet, before:

CASSIDY: Ew . . .

(River startles.)

RIVER: AH! OH MY / GOD!
CASSIDY: Oh my God, chill out! It's just me—
RIVER: Cassidy! How long have you been standing there?
CASSIDY: Like five minutes. Relax. *(Beat)* You and Uncle Frank are in the room Ainsley and I were supposed to be in.
RIVER: I'm . . . sorry?—

CASSIDY: It's okay but now my family and I have to all share the same bedroom and it's so hot and uncomfortable on the floor and I can't sleep and so I was texting with my best friend Jessica, who has insomnia, too, but my parents were like, "The light from your phone is keeping us up!" And I was like, "I can't sleep!" So they were like, "Then go somewhere!" And I was like, "Fine!" And they've been getting on my nerves all day. So I came down here. Where did you get those?

RIVER: Uh—

CASSIDY: It's okay. I've already seen them. I was there when we found them.

RIVER: . . . Your Uncle Franz was supposed to throw them away but . . . I don't know.

CASSIDY (*Coming around to sit next to River*): Are you going to keep them? They're so creepy.

RIVER (*Clutching the book*): I don't know.

CASSIDY (*Referring to River hiding the book from her*): Don't be so weird. I already saw them, I told you. You can keep looking. I'm just going to sit here.

(*Beat, as River starts looking at the photos again.*
Cassidy pretends for a moment to be dealing with something on her phone before she starts to peek at the book again.)

Why do you think Grandpa had these? Aren't these like . . . racist?

RIVER: I don't know.

CASSIDY: Do you think he was racist?

RIVER: I didn't really know your grandpa.

CASSIDY (*Prepping something on her phone*): Me neither. It was so weird going through all of his stuff today. I kept being like, "This guy was related to me?" Like, what the eff? It's so weird you can be related to someone you've never met—or like a stranger, basically—and like just because you share some genetic material? Like what if you just randomly happen to share the same exact amount of genetic material with a totally random person on the street—which probably totally happens all the time—you can't call them Grandpa. You know what I mean? Like, it's so weird—

(Cassidy tries to take a photo of the photos with her phone. River stops her.)

RIVER: Whoa—what are you doing?!

CASSIDY: Instagramming?

RIVER: Cassidy, you can't do that!

CASSIDY: Do what?

RIVER: Just, like, force your friends to look at something like this!

CASSIDY: You're looking at them . . .

RIVER: That doesn't mean everyone in the world needs to see them—I'm *making a choice* to look at them.

CASSIDY: Fine, never mind. *(Beat)* It's probably good you're keeping these though. They might be worth something.

RIVER: Really?

CASSIDY: Yeah. You can sell anything on the internet. *(Unlocks her phone, starts googling)* Let's find out. What do I search for? *(Googling)* "Antique dead people photos." *(Beat, as something loads)* There's definitely stuff . . . Victorian photos . . . post-mortem photos . . . *(Reads, then unsatisfied, types)* . . . dead black people . . . *(Off River's reaction)* What? They are black. *(Something loads)* Same stuff. Oh, duh— *(Typing)* ". . . African-American." *(Beat, something loads)* Who is Emmett Till?

RIVER *(With the photos, rapt)*: I don't know . . .

CASSIDY *(Reading something)*: "Lynching"? *(Reads, clicks, something else loads)* OMG—Bingo! Look! There are some on eBay!

(Excitedly, Cassidy tries to show River, but River isn't listening, engulfed as she is in looking.
Beat, as Cassidy clicks through her own photos online.)

These are so creepy . . . *(Finds something, shows it to River)*
OMG, look—look at that little girl in the crowd in this
one—she's, like, smiling at us!

RIVER *(Overwhelmed, closing the album)*: Okay! I think we should
stop—

CASSIDY: Why?

RIVER: They're just upsetting and I don't think we should be
looking at them anymore.

CASSIDY *(Picking up the album to leaf through)*: But I'm not
upset. *(Beat, off River's gaze)* Am I supposed to be?

RIVER *(Exasperated)*: I don't know, Cassidy.

(Beat, as Cassidy closes the album.)

CASSIDY: Where is Uncle Franz?

RIVER: Upstairs.

CASSIDY: This trip has become so stupid. The whole point was
to learn more about Daddy's family and all I've learned is
that everything is a secret.

RIVER: He's having trouble sleeping, too, and so I decided to
give him some space. It's been a big day for him.

CASSIDY: Yeah, it's so crazy he's here.

(Lying) Why did he disappear from the family again?
I always forget.

RIVER *(Suspicious)*: Uh, I don't know . . . You should ask your
parents.

(Beat.)

CASSIDY: Do you know why Aunt Toni left today?

RIVER *(Shakes her head, then)*: You should ask your parents.

CASSIDY *(A little angry)*: Ugh, why? They never tell me anything. No one ever does.

RIVER: I'm sorry—

CASSIDY: You should be. You're retarding my development. *(Sniffing the candle)* Why are you wasting these candles? Doesn't this lamp work?

(Cassidy turns the lamp on.)

RIVER *(Turns the lamp off)*: Yes, but I prefer candlelight.

CASSIDY: Why?

RIVER: I feel safer with candlelight.

CASSIDY: Safe from what?

RIVER: You don't find this house a little creepy? With that graveyard out there? All those old bones in the ground. You don't think it could be a little haunted?

(Beat.)

CASSIDY: Ghosts are for children.

RIVER: You're a children.

CASSIDY: I'm a teenager—and what do ghosts have to do with candles?

RIVER: They say, if you hold your breath and keep still and a flame flickers, it means there are spirits present.

(They stare at the candle's flame.)

CASSIDY: Or a draft.

RIVER: Okay, so you're a little know-it-all.

CASSIDY: I know there are things called science and logic.

RIVER: Science can't explain everything.

CASSIDY: Yeah it can.

RIVER: It can't tell us why we laugh.

CASSIDY: Uh, we laugh because something's funny?—

RIVER: Yeah, but why does it come out like a laugh. Why doesn't it come out like a scream or a sigh? Or why does water pour out of our face when we're sad? Why do we dream? Science still doesn't know the answer to that.

CASSIDY: And you think ghosts are the answers.

RIVER: I think the universe is full of mysteries we'll never fully comprehend and we delude ourselves into thinking otherwise but that if we respect the mystery and open ourselves up to it, the universe can sometimes reveal its truer self to us and even deeper mysteries.

CASSIDY: Whatever . . .

RIVER: Like this house. Sometimes a place can have its own spirit. A house this old can hold all sorts of things—not just ghosts—bad energies, memories. Who knows what happens when we're not here? Who knows what's happening right now that we can't even see . . . or hear? The problem is we don't know how to listen—or have forgotten how to listen. Maybe this house is trying to say something to us right now, Cassidy. Listen. What's it saying?

(There is a scratching and banging on the door, which startles the girls. Then the sound of keys being dropped is heard.)

TONI *(From off)*: Shit.

(The door opens. It's Toni.)

CASSIDY: Aunt Toni?

RIVER: Toni! You scared us—

TONI: Good. *(Referring to the order)* What is happening here?

RIVER: Oh! Rachael and I set everything up for the sale tomorrow! With everyone pitching in, it only took a few hours.

TONI *(Fake)*: Great . . .

RIVER: The only room we still have left to clear out is your father's bedroom. Rhys said he wasn't feeling well so we left him alone in there to rest—

(Toni notices Cassidy with the photo album and snatches it away.)

TONI: Cassidy, *what* are you doing with this?!
RIVER *(Confused)*: / Uhhhh—
TONI: You know you are not supposed to see these!

(Beat.)

CASSIDY: PLEASE DON'T TELL MY PARENTS!
RIVER *(Realizing Cassidy lied)*: I'm sorry, I was down here looking at them and she walked in and—
TONI: And what are you doing with them?
RIVER: I was supposed to throw them away but I thought I would
hang on to them—
TONI: Nothing here is yours "to hang on to"!
CASSIDY: Don't be mad at Aunt River! It's my fault—I just
didn't think it was fair that Rhys got to see them and not
me! I'm almost an adult—
RIVER: Cassidy actually was being very mature—asking all the
right questions. She was using the internet. She even figured out that they might be worth a little money.

(Beat.)

TONI *(Suspicious, handing photos off)*: Cassidy, go put these in
my car . . .
CASSIDY: Why?
TONI: *(Not taking her eyes off River)*: Because your "Aunties"
need to talk. You're lucky I think you're smarter than your
parents think you are but these are not appropriate for a
thirteen year old—I don't care how adult you think you
are! And I've had enough of your mother's hysterics for
the day. Now put these in my car and stay away and then
you get your butt to bed—

(Toni raises her keys over her head and presses some sort of button, tipsily. A car alarm goes off. It takes a try or two before Toni fixes this and seems to unlock the door. Cassidy takes the photos and exits through the front door.)

RIVER *(Sweetly)*: Someone's been having a good time—

TONI: All right, River, what's your real name?

RIVER: I'm sorry.

TONI: Frank just came back here calling himself stupid, so he had to get that idea from somewhere, and I know your lawyer parents did not name you River. What is your name?

(Beat.)

RIVER: Well, since you asked, I used to go by Trisha but I changed it after I—

TONI: Okay, Trisha—what are you still doing here?

RIVER: / Uh—

TONI: Because I seem to remember your visit's purpose being about an apology, which already happened, and yet I come back and you're still here having "Antiques Roadshow"—

RIVER: Do you really think we drove all the way down here to make a fuss over some old junk? Franz is here to heal himself and I'm just here to support him. And whether or not you choose to forgive him is on you—but he's made the effort. That's what counts. Now all that's left is to see the house go tomorrow—

TONI *(Skeptical)*: And why would you two need to see that?

RIVER: Because Franz is in pain—he is mourning—not just for his father but his whole life—and he didn't even get the closure of a funeral like you all did. He is stuck here and, sometimes, the only way to move forward is with a little ritual. Even if you have to sort of cobble it together for yourself. We can't go back and change the past—we can't unhurt each other, we can't unfeel feelings—but we ease the pain of the present by enacting the eternal rites.

And sometimes these rites can be as big as seeing your childhood home go or as small as an apology. *(Starts following Toni around the room)* "I'm sorry" is one of the oldest rituals we have. Did you know the root of "sorry" is actually "sore"? When you're saying "I'm sorry," you're literally saying "I'm sore." We acknowledge the reality of each other's suffering and, by the extension, the universality of suffering. We give our suffering up to the collective and we move on. Isn't that beautiful?

TONI *(Yawns, then)*: How's your mother, Trisha?

RIVER: She's fine . . .

TONI: Oh okay, because, by the time I was your age, mine was dead and it was a very ugly and slow and painful death that I was forced to watch very closely. And then I was forced to watch my father and his two little boys mourn her, which is a different kind of pain. In fact, I watched my father mourn her for the rest of his life. And then I watched him die. So I don't need you to come in here with your "old soul" giving me your notes from your hippy dippy community college anthro seminar on grief and suffering and mourning because I know all those girls personally and it takes more than a little ritual to send them away. It takes time, which you—fortunately or unfortunately—know next to nothing about.

RIVER: You're right, Toni. I'm sorry. Franz has told me all about what happened here and you were the one who had to deal with so much of it. Family can be so hard on us women. You were something of a mother to him, weren't you? Now I understand how hard this is for you. My mother had a very difficult time when I came home to make amends. But you know what I think might help? *(Touching her)* A sister. I have three and you wouldn't imagine the difference it makes—

TONI *(Horrified)*: You know what's going to help? You getting the hell away from me! *(Beat)* I think I just figured you out. You're one of those "Sweet Girls," aren't you? Do people ever call you that? Do people look at you and go, "Aw, River, you're so sweet!" I haven't seen one of you in a long time. In fact, I wonder if I used to be one of you. I think I remember running around being "sweet" and twenty-three, thinking I knew everything and was gonna save everybody by "loving" them into submission. God. But you know what happens to Sweet Girls? Life gobbles you up—faster than the other girls. And why? Because we run around putting a target on our backs, looking so tasty, sprinkling our sugar over all the world's shit. But let me tell you now what no one ever told me: you don't get an unlimited supply. That sugar is gonna run out. So don't be in such a hurry to waste it on Frank. You're not going to fix him. I tried—this whole family's tried—but Frank is going to be who he is, which is a grown man and a hot dog mess. So take my advice: save some of this sweetness for yourself—save some of you for you.

RIVER: No offense, Toni, but you and I are not the same person and Franz has got sweetness in him, too—

TONI: No, honey, Frank has got a sweet tooth—

RIVER: And what we have is love—real love—and that is not something that runs out—

TONI *(Getting up to go)*: Okay, honey—

RIVER: And I'm having his baby—

TONI: All right, good luck with that—

RIVER: No, Toni. I don't think you get it. I'm actually pregnant.

(Toni freezes.)

TONI: What?

RIVER *(Relieved)*: I found out a few days ago . . . You're the first person I've told. I haven't even told Franz. I'm going to tell him here. It's actually the end of this whole journey I've planned. Tomorrow, after everything is over—once he's . . . seen this house go—we're going to camp out somewhere around here in these woods—pitch a tent under the stars, build a fire, meditate, sing some songs, and reconnect with this old Earth—and, right at the end, right before we go to bed, that's when I'm going to tell him—let him fall asleep feeling how his life is really going to change. And I'd like for you to be a part of this child's life. I'd like for everyone here to be a part of its life. But I can't make you. Though you and Bo are both parents. You know what it takes to be one. Franz doesn't. He's going to need help. His mother died when he was a boy. His father couldn't raise him. Don't you think Franz could use your help? Don't you think this child could use a father who knows what the love of family is?

TONI: Do you even know what he did here?

RIVER: I do, Toni. And I don't care. I was a young girl once. I remember what the attentions of an older man could feel like then. I remember what it was to want to feel grown up. Look at your niece. And I'm not excusing what he did, but I do think that there are gray areas. And I also think that people make mistakes and deserve to be forgiven, when they ask for it. And I also think that people can really change. I believe that. Why don't you?

TONI: Oh my goodness—

(Bo comes down the stairs, heavily. He sees Toni and freezes.)

BO: Toni? *(Beat)* Where the heck have you been?

TONI: I've been out.

BO: Have you been drinking?

TONI: Sure have.

BO: Alone?

TONI: Nope. I found a friend. Since I don't have any in this house.

RIVER: I'm gonna leave you two alone . . . *(To Toni)* Let's keep that between us girls, okay?

(River exits.)

TONI: She's pregnant.

BO: What?

TONI: She and Frank are going to have a baby—

BO: What am I supposed to do with this information?

TONI: What am I supposed to do with it? At first, I thought she was just some sort of sneaky, evil . . . vegan—but now I'm beginning to think that maybe she's just an idiot kid. She just stood there and told me she was totally okay with the fact that Frank was a pedophile—she's carrying a pedophile's baby!

BO: Toni—

TONI (*Realizing*): Wait—unless she was lying! Bo, did she just fake that pregnancy?

BO: Toni, I just spent the whole day here with the two of them. Their intentions are genuine. The man only came all the way down here to apologize. Why can't you just accept it?

TONI: Because it's not real. I'm sorry, but I've seen this before. You've just never been around for it. I heard the apology when he totaled every car we let him drive. I heard the apology when he got caught at the pharmacy sneaking off with Vicodin and the sheriff let him off for some god-awful reason. I heard the apology when that little girl's redneck family came in here threatening Daddy with all that nonsense, throwing bricks through the windows— Jesus. I heard the apology when we found all those nasty pictures on his computer—

BO: It been ten years, Toni.

TONI: Yes, ten years of relief. Relief! In his absence, I felt relief. And don't act like you didn't either—you've never once worried about him once the entire time he was gone—

BO: That's not true!

TONI: You never mentioned him once—

BO: Neither did you!

TONI: Because I didn't think you cared.

(*Beat.*)

BO: Who were you with just now?

TONI: I was with Juanita.

BO: You got drunk with our father's nurse?

TONI: I needed to be with somebody who might have actually liked our father—maybe even missed him. I was beginning to think I'd hallucinated a father. And she called him one of the nicest gentlemen she'd ever worked for? And she's never seen the photos before. She didn't know what I was even talking about—

BO: Because he would have showed her the pictures?

TONI: And didn't think he was a racist—and she's black!

BO: You actually asked her that? She was our employee. What else was she going to say? Why are you acting like our father was some freedom fighter when you know he wasn't?

TONI: Then what was he, Bo.

BO: I don't know but know he wasn't a saint. And I know this is probably all a little hard for you to receive, because you were his favorite, but—

TONI: What are you talking about I was his favorite!?

BO: Come on. You were Dad's favorite just like I was Mom's favorite?

TONI: You were *Mom's* fav—*did you just appoint yourself that?* (*Beat, exasperated*) Oh God. (*Beat*) And whose favorite was Frank?

BO: I always thought he was your favorite.

TONI: If Daddy had a favorite, it was him. You know, when he first went missing, I thought he was dead? I worried myself nearly to death. But then I found out the receipts from the wires Daddy had been sending him. Frank was writing home for money. Daddy was giving it to him. And they were both keeping it from me—from me! After all I'd done.

BO: How long ago was this?

TONI: Five, six years ago. After all the life I wasted—the worry— they kept it from me. So I thought, fine. And I took that life back. That worry turned to relief. A person is born

71

with only a certain amount of energy, I realized. And you can waste it on the wrong person and the wrong things. I should have been raising my own child when I was raising someone else's.

(Beat.)

BO: I shouldn't have said that about Rhys—
TONI: Then why did you say it?
BO: You were being so . . . cruel.
TONI: Do you think I am a bad mother?
BO: No.
TONI: Then why doesn't he want to be with me? *(Beat)* Can you believe I was actually looking forward to this weekend? I thought it was going to be fun. I don't know what exactly I thought was going to happen. I guess maybe we were just going to go through Daddy's stuff, maybe swap stories about him—about each other—tell them to our kids. Somehow we would keep him alive that way. But nobody here cares about any of that. People seem happy that he's dead.
BO: No one is happy that he's dead.
TONI: Oh, really? Because the only thing upsetting you seems to be your bank account—
BO: I'm about to lose my job, Toni.
TONI: What?
BO: I think. I have a feeling corporate is about to close us down. This is why I've been on the phone all weekend. Rachael doesn't know so please keep that to yourself. So I really can't afford any of this. If it happens, I don't know what I'm going to do.

(Beat.)

TONI: Did you ever think maybe Daddy wanted us to lose the place?

BO: What?

TONI: Juanita thinks that Daddy hid the notices from the banks—that's why I never saw them. She says she sees it all the time, that he was probably ashamed of the mess he made and didn't want us to be bothered with any of it. Maybe we were supposed to lose it. Maybe he wanted us to let it go.

(Beat.)

BO: How did we ever sign on to this nonsense?

TONI: We thought it would give the two of them something to do.

BO: Who were these morons that Dad thought who would be like, "You know where I've always wanted to vacation? Arkansas! Let's find a little B&B somewhere in Arkansas and stay there for the weekend!"

TONI: This place has its charms. You've just always been a brat about it.

BO: What are you talking / about?

TONI: You're the reason we stopped coming in the summers— Mommy and Daddy were tired of watching you sulk and complain all day—

BO: Well, sorry my idea of fun wasn't . . . killing some animal or Grandma's endless stories about some Great-Great-Great-Cousin-Bubba hiding sacks of flour from the Yankees or whatever—no air-conditioning—and if you said anything about it, people told you to go jump in that disgusting lake. "Go take a cool dip in the lake if ya get hot!" That cesspool—covered in algae and they treated it like Niagara frickin' Falls—I just didn't get it—I just didn't effin' get it—bugs everywhere—what did you like about it?!

TONI: I don't know. I always liked Grandma's stories. Though I can't remember any of them now. But I sort of get what Daddy was trying to do. Those cousins were just letting it fall apart. This place has history—our history. He wanted to honor it. It had value to him.

BO: Value. Look at this place. You think Dad had any idea what half of this junk was?

(Rachael comes downstairs.)

RACHAEL: Bo!—

(Rachael sees Bo and Toni. She freezes. There is a seething between the two women.)

BO: Sorry—I got distracted—

RACHAEL: Fine. I'll get them. But I'm getting sleepy, so . . .

(Rachael exits into the kitchen.)

TONI: What's happening?

BO *(Pulls out a bottle in his pocket)*: We're having a nightcap, but it's hard to sneak with the kids. You want some? It's good.

TONI: No, no, don't let me crash the celebration—

BO: What?

TONI *(Referring to the order)*: The takeover.

BO: What? No, Toni, this is just like a little ritual we do. *(Gesturing to the house)* You know, I think Rachael actually did all this because she wants to make up.

TONI: Oh—not to prove she's better than me?!

BO: Please just apologize? I don't want to choose sides.

TONI: Tell me to my face that you don't think Daddy is a bigot.

(Beat.)

BO: Do you remember dropping me off in New Haven my freshman year?

TONI: Yes. Mom was so sick she couldn't leave the car.

BO: Well, we showed up at my quad that I'm sharing with three other guys and lo and behold one of my roommates is this black kid from Philly. This nice, bright kid, Clarence Montgomery. I even remember his name. The quad was split into two bedrooms, two guys each bunking up, and for whatever reason we were the last to arrive and the only bed left was with Clarence. And while you and Mom sat in the car, Daddy and I set about unpacking and the whole time, he wouldn't look Clarence in the face—he was so uncomfortable—

TONI: Daddy's discomfort around your college roommate is not the / same thing—

BO: And right before he left, Daddy pulls me aside and says, "You keep an eye on your stuff." And I see he's looking at Clarence, who's not even paying attention to us. "Be careful," Daddy said. Now why would Dad say something like that to me?

TONI: Bo, it was a different time. These things were still so new! He was anxious.

BO: But how do we know he ever stopped being . . . anxious? *(Beat)* Though, I guess, now we'll never know. *(Beat)* How are you dealing with the pictures by the way—with Rhys?

TONI: What do you mean?

BO: Didn't he see them?

TONI: What's there to deal with? I'm sure he's had this in a history class.

BO: I don't remember reading about these in any history class. Though I'm trying to talk Rachael down from an Emergency Family Symposium on the History of America's Bullshit. I told her we should wait and see if Ainsley actually says anything. He didn't even seem to know what he was looking at. I'm just glad we threw them away.

TONI: Uh, I wouldn't be so sure. I came in just now and your pal River was sitting here on the couch looking through them.

BO: Really?

TONI: Yes. She seems to think they're worth something. She tells me she was going to "hang on to them."

BO: Frank must have given them to her.

TONI: See, Bo? They're up to / something.

BO: You know, I did think those pictures looked like some sort of weird . . . historical thing. And there's a lot of them. You think we should try to find a way to sell them tomorrow? Or, I don't know. Maybe we should talk to someone.

TONI: Do you ever stop working?

BO: Shut up. Where are they?

TONI: I put them in my car.

(Rachael reenters from the kitchen with a glass of water. Bo and Toni notice. Beat.)

RACHAEL: Bo . . .

(Bo gets up to exit. Rhys is seen at the top of the stairs, carrying his pillow, the quilt.)

BO: Go to bed.

RACHAEL: Where is our daughter?

BO: Who knows? Let's do this—

RACHAEL *(Seeing Rhys)*: Hi, Rhys. Feeling better?

(Rhys nods. Rachael and Bo exit.)

TONI: Are you sick?

RHYS: No but I had to tell them something so they'd leave me the fuck alone—what took you so long? I thought you were coming right back!

TONI: I stopped by Juanita's.

RHYS: You stopped answering your phone.

TONI: It died—

RHYS: How could you leave me here with these awful fucking people? You should have seen Uncle Bo and Rachael bossing everyone around—nagging and whining about money as if they hadn't all just flown down here first class. I fucking hate these people.

TONI: You don't hate your family.

RHYS: I hate this family.

(Beat.)

TONI: You like Cassidy.

RHYS: She's just a kid.

TONI: But you two should know each other. One day you might need each other. For like a kidney or something. Plus I think she has a little crush on you—

RHYS: Mom, ew—

TONI: What? I'm not telling you to do anything!

RHYS: She's just really into science—

TONI: Okay—

RHYS: Whatever—did you do it or not?

TONI: I did.

RHYS: Good. That'll show Rachael, the Jew bitch.

TONI: Rhys! Where did you get that from?

RHYS: What? That's what she is! Bo, too, basically. *(Beat, noticing)* Are you drunk?

TONI: No. *(Beat)* Hey—do we need to talk about those photos you saw earlier?

RHYS: I don't know. Do we?

TONI: Do you have any questions, or . . . ?

RHYS: No. *(Beat)* Did they belong to Grandpa?

(Beat.)

TONI: I don't think so, but we actually don't know. And now we'll never know. *(Beat)* Why don't you come up and sleep in Grandpa's room with me?

RHYS: Mom, no.

(Beat.)

TONI: Do you think I'm a bad mother?

RHYS: What?

TONI: Do you?

RHYS: . . . No.

TONI: Then what is wrong? Something's wrong. Do you think I'm mad at you or something—because I'm not. I forgive you and I will always forgive you, no matter what. I'm on your side. You know that, right?

RHYS: Yes.

(Beat.)

TONI: Can I have a hug?

RHYS: Uh, sure.

(Toni embraces Rhys with intensity.)

TONI: You give good hugs.

RHYS: You're drunk.

TONI: Drunk on loving you—and I'm still going to wake up tomorrow morning and thank God for you because I love love love you. *(They disengage)* Good night.

(Toni exits. Rhys takes a minute to recover from that before he starts to set up his pallet on the couch, during which Cassidy finally emerges from the shadows.)

CASSIDY: Rhys—

RHYS *(Startled)*: Cassidy! Where did you just come from?

CASSIDY: Hey, sorry—I need your help—

RHYS *(Seeing the album in her hands)*: Are those—

CASSIDY: Grandpa's photos, yeah. I was supposed to put these in your mom's car, but she was drunk and didn't unlock it right and I can't keep them with me because I'm sharing a room with my parents and they will flip out if they see me with them, so can I just leave them with you? And in the morning, maybe you can put them in your mom's car for me?

RHYS: Uh . . . sure?

CASSIDY: You're the best. *(Beat)* Are you feeling better?

RHYS: Yeah. I just had a headache. I just needed some quiet.

CASSIDY: Yeah . . .

(Beat.)

Did you know that cicadas are the oldest bugs on earth? Or, like, they live longer than any other bugs. These bugs outside, they're thirteen years old. I just realized . . . they're as old as I am. But this is, like, the end of their life. They're about to die. Can you imagine if I just died this year? *(Beat)* And do you know why they're singing? *(Off Rhys's reaction)* It's because they're trying to find each other to mate . . . They spend like all this time underground becoming teenagers, waiting to hatch, and then they just sing for a few weeks in the summer so they can find another cicada to do it with and then they die before the children are even born? Isn't that so messed up? That this song is like the whole point of their existence . . . *(Beat)* Do you think I have a crush on you?

RHYS: I hope not . . .

CASSIDY: Yeah . . . How do you think the baby cicadas learn the song? Is it just something that's programmed in them? Or maybe they just pick it up somewhere, listening when they're eggs. Maybe they're hearing it in their sleep, and that's how they learn? And their parents are dead, but they have this memory of a song that they think is just a part of them . . .

RHYS: Cassidy, did you hear something?

CASSIDY: Hear what? Sorry I'm being so weird. I think it's this place. Do you believe in ghosts?

RHYS: What?

CASSIDY: Or I think I'm just upset. Maybe it's the photos. *(Jumps up, maybe genuinely upset)* See you in the morning.

RHYS: Good night.

(Cassidy exits upstairs. Rhys is left with the album of photos. He goes over to the couch, and sits down with them. He starts looking through them. There is a long while of Rhys looking at the photos, sort of distractedly. After a while, he puts the open photograph album to the side and stares into space, thinking. He tries to sleep. He can't. He takes out his phone. He clicks around on it. Something comes up and he plays it. The sound of two men having sex is heard coming from the phone. Embarrassed, he puts his phone on mute quickly, checks to see if anyone heard, then, keeping his eyes on the screen, he puts his hand down his pants and starts masturbating. The open photograph album is uncomfortably close by. This goes on for a little bit before Franz enters from upstairs, pulling a cigarette out of a pack. Seeing Rhys, he freezes on the steps. There is a moment of confusion, panic and embarrassment, which traps Franz on the stairs for a moment. He spins in a circle, unsure what to do, until he decides to just—)

FRANZ: Hey, Rhys?

(Quickly, Rhys stops what he's doing, turns off the phone and hides it somewhere.)

RHYS: Hey—yeah?

(Franz comes downstairs over the following and stands next to Rhys, examining the scene.)

FRANZ: What's going on dude?

RHYS: Nothing. You?

FRANZ: Just going for a smoke, if that's okay. Can't sleep. You feeling better?

RHYS: Yeah. Just . . . just trying to get some sleep myself.

FRANZ: You sleep sitting up, or . . . ?

RHYS: Ha, no! I was just thinking . . .

(Franz notices the open photograph album next to Rhys. Beat, before:)

FRANZ *(Awkward)*: Are those the—?

RHYS *(Lying, casually flipping through them)*: Yeah . . . I was just, um, looking at them . . .

(Beat, in which Franz puts something together which is not altogether accurate. He seems to struggle internally for a second before making a choice:)

FRANZ *(Awkwardly)*: Okay dude—you know what? . . . I totally saw what you were doing— *(Off Rhys's reaction)* But I'm not trying to embarrass you or anything! I just feel like maybe I should—we should be talking—like I feel like we have a lot in common? Like I heard about what happened at your school with the drugs and like now I'm seeing this and I actually have a similar like—well not really because you're—okay, the point is that there's a thing and it's cool and what am I trying to say? *(Beat)* Okay, you know, it's like . . . you know, who are we, you know? We're just these bundles of nerves and feelings and confusion and we have so little in our possession to actually help us deal with ourselves or any of these things and like, you know? And it's so confusing. But I just wanted to say, like, you shouldn't feel ashamed, you know what I mean? Because, you know, if you want, there are ways to, you know, sort of . . . rewire yourself? If you want? Because, like, we're humans. And that's what humans can do . . .

RHYS *(Not really sure what's going on)*: Uh-huh . . .

FRANZ: Like, okay, I don't know how much your mom has—did your mom tell you about why I left?

RHYS: Not really—

FRANZ: Okay! Well, I actually struggled for a long time with something, I guess, similar, you know—just like really disturbing stuff—or stuff certain people might find disturbing—and it started with just like stupid shit I found on the internet—I was looking at stuff I shouldn't have been looking at and not being careful about what I was attaching my . . . feeling to—and, you know, it became kind of an addiction. And it got to a point where I thought this thing was, like, some really awful part of me that I would never—like some sort of . . . but it's not, you know? It's not You . . . *(Pointing at Rhys)* You . . . are not your urges. *You* are bigger than them—I mean, there's nothing *wrong* with being . . . with having Urges—everyone's got urges—but if you don't like yours . . . like, you can be "normal," if you want, you know? I mean, what is normal, but you know? There are other ways to, you know, be . . . You don't have to feel trapped is what I'm saying. Am I making any sense? *(Beat—maybe no reaction from Rhys)* God, River is so much better at this sort of thing than me. When she came into my life, she really helped me find the strength to . . . deal with myself? And realize my potential. And it wasn't until she came along that I realized that was something I never had. And maybe you never had that, either, because our family is kind of messed up . . . *(Off Rhys's blank stare)* But, you know what? I'm gonna do that for you now.

RHYS *(Not sure what's going on)*: You . . . are?

FRANZ *(Pointing to the photos)*: I'm gonna take these. If that's okay with you.

RHYS *(Completely confused)*: Yeah, sure. I mean . . . I'm supposed to put them in Mom's car so . . .

FRANZ *(Taking the photos)*: It's okay . . . I'll take care of them . . . *(Beat)* Wait—do you actually even remember me? You were just a kid, but do you remember—

RHYS: Yeah—at Christmas you would come . . .

FRANZ: Okay, okay, cool. *(Beat)* Hey, do I seem different to you?

RHYS: Not really. A little older.

FRANZ: Okay . . . Yeah, okay.

(Franz exits. Alone, Rhys is confused, mortified, any number of things. He lays down on the couch and pulls the quilt up over himself, trying to figure out what just happened. He eventually puts it together. It's painful.

Curtain. Cicadas.)

ACT THREE

The Book of Genesis

1

The living room, the next morning.

Day reveals the extent to which the place has been completely organized. Neatness abounds. Ray's remaining possessions are displayed and arranged about like the organs of a dissected animal. The order is almost oppressive. It's like a museum. Or a mausoleum.

Rhys is a blanketed figure on the couch, again. Rachael sits on the sofa's arm near his head. River stands nearby with a cup of tea. Occasionally, we hear the sounds of Cassidy and Ainsley in the next room, playing some sort of rowdy game that involves counting, screaming and laughter.

RACHAEL *(Trying gently to wake Rhys up)*: Rhys . . .
RHYS: Hm—huh?

RACHAEL: Hey, sweetie, I'm sorry to wake you up, but I think it's going to get a little busy down here in a bit. Do you want to go sleep in our bedroom?

RHYS: I should get up . . .

RACHAEL: Okay . . . And do you know when the estate sale is supposed to start? I don't know if your mother gave these people a specific time or not . . .

RHYS: No . . .

RACHAEL: Okay . . . *(Beat)* Would you mind asking your mother for me?

RHYS *(Falling back asleep)*: Okay . . .

(Beat.)

RACHAEL: Could you do that now, honey?

(Rhys finally stands up, grumpily, and exits slowly up the stairs.)

(To River) See? Sometimes these Lafayette boys just need a little push.

(Rhys, hearing this, flips Rachael off behind her back before exiting. Bo wanders in from somewhere, hanging up his phone and dialing a new number.)

Any luck?

BO: He just gave me some other guy's number to call. Hold on.

(Bo wanders out on to the porch.)

RIVER: What's going on?

RACHAEL: He's talking to someone about the photos. And thank you by the way— *(Needing help, referring to a couch)* Can you—?

RIVER: Oh, sure!—

(Over the following, they push the couch against the wall to clear the floor, then they set up another table where the couch was.)

RACHAEL: When Bo told me he tried to throw these pictures away, I almost killed him. I told him we have to deal with these things. We should sit down with them and the kids and really unpack what is going on. Especially after Rhys had seen them, because, you know, kids talk. Ainsley's one thing—if we're lucky he'll forget all about—but Cassidy is the one to worry about. If she wants to see something, she will go after it. And if she saw those pictures without me, I literally might have to kill her and then kill myself. She's at such an impressionable age.

(They're done.)

RIVER: Can I just say we are both amazing?
RACHAEL: We are. Look at this. Thank you so much for your help.
RIVER: This was all you.
RACHAEL: Well, it was mostly for my own sanity. After those photos, the last thing I needed was for someone to find a . . . jar of . . . penises or something.
RIVER: What?
RACHAEL: Bo and I spent all night reading about these awful lynchings and apparently, it was customary for people take souvenirs after these killings—ears, fingers, genitals— *(Poking her head in the den)* HEY! KEEP IT DOWN IN THERE! YOUR AUNT TONI IS STILL SLEEPING!

*(The noise quiets down—for a little while.
Rachael starts arranging things on the new table.
Bo wanders through.)*

BO: Uh-huh . . . Well, I haven't gotten a good look, but I'd say at least forty, fifty, sixty pictures . . . / Uh-huh . . .

(Bo wanders out just as Toni comes stalking downstairs. She is clearly hungover. Beat, as the women look at each other.)

RIVER: Good morning, Toni!
RACHAEL: Toni, what time is the sale supposed to start?

(Unresponsive, Toni exits into the kitchen.)

RIVER: I think she's hungover.
RACHAEL *(Goes over to the den)*: Cassidy?

(Cassidy enters from the den, wearing something crazy on her head like a lampshade.)

CASSIDY: What?!
RACHAEL *(Taking the thing off her head)*: What are you two doing?
CASSIDY: We're playing ghosts!
RACHAEL: Well don't play that! Your Aunt Toni is finally up. I need you to take your brother upstairs and the two of you finish cleaning out your grandfather's room.
CASSIDY: Ugh!—
RACHAEL: Just do it! / And quickly!

(Cassidy stomps upstairs, Ainsley in tow.)

CASSIDY *(From off)*: OKAY! JESUS!

(Bo pokes his head in from the porch and motions to everyone to keep it down.)

BO: I guess some of them looked like postcards, / but some were like, photo-photos . . . Is there a difference? I'd have to look again . . .

(Bo wanders back out onto the porch, just as Toni reenters with a cup of coffee.)

RACHAEL: Hi. Let me know when you're done acting like a child, so we can finish what we all came here to do.

(Toni takes her time sitting down on the couch. She takes her time taking a sip of coffee. She clears her throat.)

BO *(From the porch)*: You're kidding! / Oh my God—no, that's good to know!

TONI *(To River)*: Good morning, Trisha. *(Beat)* And, Rachael, you can stop whatever you're doing because I canceled the sale.

RACHAEL: Excuse me?

TONI: And the auction. And I pulled down all the notices for the sale yesterday—or all the ones I could find—and had the local paper print something up. There may still be some stragglers but, just in case, I put a little sign down the road that says: SALE CANCELED DUE TO CRISIS OF FAMILY. So . . . thanks for nothing.

(Bo reenters, hanging up the phone, a smile on his face.)

BO: Hey—when are we starting?

RACHAEL: Uh, never. Because your sociopath of a sister went behind our backs and canceled everything after we worked our asses off trying to help clean up the mess she made!

TONI: Rachael, did someone *ask* for your help?

BO: Hey! Okay. Okay. Rachael, relax—

RACHAEL: What do you mean relax?! Your sister is . . . a—a fucking cunt!!!

TONI: Rachael, your language!

RACHAEL: I don't care! In fact, let's make this a teaching moment! Bring Ainsley on down here so he can look at you and learn what the definition of a fucking cunt is, you sabotaging fucking cunt!

(Quietly, Rhys entered from upstairs and stands on the steps. Toni sees him and winks.)

BO: Rachael, Rachael, Rachael—it doesn't matter.

RACHAEL: What are you talking about!?

BO: It wasn't going to make a difference anyway. The bank can have it all. *(Beat)* River, I could kiss you!

RACHAEL: / What?

TONI: What?

BO: Toni, after our conversation last night, I thought it might be worth trying to get a real appraisal of these pictures, and I just got off the phone with a friend of a friend, who explained to me that these photos are like . . . highly specialized collector's items—like antiques—Daddy was sitting on a gold mine—and if we did this right, through an actual auction house or a private dealer, we're looking at the upper six figures here—maybe more!

TONI: What?

BO: Right? So can you go get them out of your car and bring them here? I need to take a look at them and make a quick count. This guy's waiting for me to call him back with a number, so he can start reaching out to some people he thinks might be interested in this stuff—

RACHAEL: What kind of people?

BO: I don't know but, in the meantime, I was thinking it might make the most sense for me to take them back to New York tonight. The best appraisers for this are obviously in the city—

RIVER: Uh, and what about Franz?

(Beat, in which Bo and Toni look at River.)

BO: What about Franz?

RIVER: Was he going to be a part of this conversation? Technically, he's entitled to a third of those pictures.

BO: Well, first we're going to get through today, then we'll talk about who gets what—

RIVER: That's fine but if you're taking those photos back with you, it sounds like you're not declaring those as a part of your father's estate—and that's what Franz is legally entitled to and that's what's getting liquidated today. So this is a little shady . . .

(Beat.)

TONI: Rhys, sweetie, will you go get the photos out of my car?

(Rhys exits.)

(To River) I thought y'all weren't here for money—

RIVER: That doesn't mean Franz shouldn't have a say in what happens with his father's things.

TONI: It seems to me if Frank actually had something to say, he'd be here. Where is he?

RIVER: I haven't seen him since I woke up this morning. Why don't I call him?

TONI: Why don't you do that?

(River takes out her phone, walking into the corner the way people do when they're on a call. Beat, while it rings. Franz's voicemail picks up.)

RIVER: Hey, baby. / It's me. I don't know where you are but you should come back to the house. There's a little problem you need to be a part of, so come on back. I hope you're having a beautiful time, whatever you're doing. I love you. See you soon.

TONI *(To Bo)*: See!? Her pregnancy and her lawyer parents— it's a trick! She's here for money and there is no way! If

Frank makes a dime off of this after all he's taken, I will just die, Bo!

BO: We're talking about a substantial amount of money here! There's more than enough for everyone. There's no reason to toss this away out / of spite.

TONI: Money is the problem, Bo! I canceled everything just for this reason! All this stress over money is what's destroying this family! Don't you see? Daddy wanted us to lose the house—Daddy wanted us to just start over—and I mean, given we aren't 100% sure that these photos are even Daddy's, there should be another way—

RACHAEL (*Under her breath*): Jesus Christ.

RIVER: I left him a voice mail.

(They both realize River is off the phone and that she has been standing there, listening.)

TONI: Great, well, we've decided we're not selling the pictures. We're going to find something else to do with them—maybe we can donate them to a museum or something—

BO: Toni, you are going to have nothing to do with these!—

TONI: I'm the executor, Bo.

BO: If you think you are about to hold those things hostage, you have got another thing coming. I will sue you!

(Rhys reenters, empty-handed.)

RHYS: Ummm . . .

BO: Where are they?

RHYS: I couldn't find them.

BO: What do you mean you couldn't find them? I thought you said you put them in your car!

TONI (*Looking at River*): We did.

BO (*Notices the look, then to River*): Okay, where are they?!

RIVER: How should I know?

BO: All right, clearly you and Toni were the last people to see these things—correct?

RIVER: Okay?

BO: And weren't you the one who told Toni they were worth something and that you were going to hang onto them?

RIVER: I'm sorry, are you implying that I stole them?

BO: I'm not implying anything, but I think it might be a good idea if you brought down your luggage so we can just be sure. Look, trust me, I know how expensive a baby is—I've had two—and you probably need the money—I get it—

RACHAEL: / Bo, calm down, come on—

RIVER *(Looking at Toni, betrayed)*: Whoa! Whoa! Whoa! First of all—your daughter was the last person with the photos!

RACHAEL: / What?

BO *(Spinning around to see her)*: What?!

RIVER: Last night. Toni caught Cassidy and I looking at the photos and she told her to take them outside.

(Beat.)

RACHAEL: What?!

BO: CASSIDY GET DOWN HERE RIGHT NOW!

RACHAEL *(To River)*: You and my daughter were looking at the—and you didn't *tell me*?!

BO: Rachael, please!—

(Cassidy comes down the stairs.)

CASSIDY: What's going on!?

RACHAEL: DID YOU SEE THE PHOTOS?!

CASSIDY: Yes?

RACHAEL *(To Bo)*: AGGHH!

CASSIDY: Mom! I don't understand what the big deal is. I've seen worse things on the internet. I am almost an adult!

BO: You are not an adult!

CASSIDY: Yes I am!

BO: / No you're not!

RACHAEL: NO YOU'RE NOT!

TONI: Can we all just calm down! Cassidy, honey, where did you put the photos? They're not in the car.

CASSIDY: They're not?

TONI: They're not there anymore.

CASSIDY *(To Rhys, sort of annoyed)*: Then Rhys has them!

(Beat. All eyes on Rhys.)

TONI: What?

(Beat.)

Okay, somebody had better start explaining something right now.

(Beat.)

RACHAEL: RIGHT! NOW!

BO: / Rachael—

CASSIDY: The car was locked and I gave them to Rhys to put in the car!

TONI: And what did you do with them Rhys?

RHYS: Uh, I—

(The front door opens and Franz enters. He is shirtless and dripping wet.)

FRANZ: Good morning, everybody!

BO: / Frank?

TONI: Ew, Frank, why are you soaking wet?

FRANZ: I've been swimming!

TONI: Swimming?

FRANZ: In the lake! Can you believe in all the years I lived here, I never once went swimming in that lake? It's amazing!

And I—I think I might have baptized myself! *(Off their reactions)* I mean, I don't know if I "baptized" myself— I don't know how people do it—but I just went to the edge of the water and said, "Water, heal me!" And it did . . . I got out of that water and I feel . . . changed. I'm literally shaking right now—oh my God—

(Beat.)

RIVER: Honey, did you take something?
FRANZ: No! No, I wish! I'm just feeling good for once!
BO: Frank, we don't have time for this. We're in the middle of a crisis—
FRANZ: What happened?
BO: The photos are missing.
FRANZ: Missing? No they're not.
BO: Well then where are they?

(Beat, as Franz takes a moment to collect himself.)

FRANZ: Okay. Where do I even start? Okay. Okay. *(Beat)* So this is going to sound a little weird, but yesterday River thinks she saw a ghost. *(Off River's reaction)* Or felt a ghost! Or a ghost felt her! A spirit! *(Off everyone's reactions)* I know, I know—but River is actually very sensitive. She's actually certified in something called / Reiki—
RIVER: Reiki.
FRANZ: And okay maybe it's not really a spirit—usually, I rag on her about it—but, yesterday, I saw it happen and— I mean, she looked really spooked—it seemed really real and then, last night, I couldn't sleep. I mean, I've had a lot of trouble sleeping these days and last night I was just lying in my childhood bed with River and I realized . . . I was feeling something, too—an old feeling—and this old feeling it was like . . . the air was like buzzing with it and I couldn't take it anymore—I couldn't breathe—so

I got out of bed and came downstairs to have a cigarette and— *(Accidental eye contact)* You know, Rhys was on the couch with the photos—you know, just looking at them— no big deal—and I was like, "He shouldn't have this!" So I took them away and, as I was leaving, I was like: "Wait. Maybe this is why I'm here." I mean, I'm here to prove that I've changed, but maybe I am being selfish, Toni. Maybe I am a taker and chaos. But I want to change and I have to be the opposite in order to be different, so I have to bring order. I have to help. So I'm thinking, you know how I'm going to help? I'm going to solve the mystery of who these belonged to, because I grew up here and I never once saw these before or saw Daddy with them and, honestly, I really can't see Daddy ever . . . having something like this—like if I'm being really honest—it's like they came from nowhere, but I guess I had this idea that I was going to figure out if Daddy or anyone in this family had anything to do with these photos. I would see if I could find the trees. I know the property well enough. If any of the trees . . . used in these pictures were on our property, I would know. So I just set out with my little iPhone flashlight and I'm looking at the photos and I'm looking at the trees and the bugs are going crazy and I mean I was out there for a while just chasing these trees when I hear a voice in my head—Daddy's voice—go, "François? What are you doing? These pictures are so old. The trees in them are probably completely different looking by now." And by the time I realize this, I also realize that I'm lost—like I don't know where I am, I don't recognize this place anymore—the trees are all different—and these cicadas are just . . . roaring—and every pine or oak or whatever is just—is just covered in these bugs—it's just terrifying—it's like the whole forest—all that darkness—it's moving—and I'm just trapped in this sound— and I'm trying to figure out where I am—trying to, like, locate myself—and, after a while, all these memories start coming back to me about this place—every memory that I've buried—memories of when I used to pace through these orchards, high or drunk out of my mind, trying to hatch some escape plan—and I'm like really scared I'm not going to get out of here alive—like my life is flashing before my eyes—like I'm going to die here—but then I look up and see I'm standing in the slave cemetery—that little clearing in the woods where all the slaves are buried.

You hardly realize you're there until you're right up on it and I'm standing in the middle of this graveyard and I was remembering all this stuff River's been saying about spirits and how we're just these porous vessels of energy susceptible to influence and we're not what we think we are and that sometimes there's this thing inside of us that's leading us and we just have to follow it and so you sometimes just have to trust it and that something led me here. And I turned around and there was the lake—the water and the sun coming up over it and it's glittering and it's calling to me and then I realized this was the whole purpose to this journey and I was lost and this thing helped me find myself and it was taking me to the edge of the water and it seemed to be telling me, "Go on in. Go in and cleanse yourself. Cleanse everyone. Wipe it all away. Take it all in with you and leave it there." So I did. I took everything—all my pain, all Daddy's pain, this family's pain, the pictures—and I left it there. I washed it away.

(Beat, in which Toni starts laughing. She continues laughing for a while and over the following.)

TONI: Frank. Those photos were worth a lot of money.
FRANZ: They were?! How much?
TONI: Hundreds of thousands of dollars. Maybe more.

(Beat.)

BO: YOU FUCKING IDIOT!

RACHAEL: / BO!

FRANZ: I didn't know they were worth money! You told me to throw them away!

BO (*About to have an aneurysm, basically*): OH MY GOD!

FRANZ: / I didn't know.

(*Toni laughs.*)

BO: OH MY GOD FRANK WHAT THE FUCK IS WRONG WITH YOU!?

RIVER: You leave him alone! How can you not see the gift he has tried to give you people! Look at the evil and rot you're descended from—and all Franz tried to do was purify you—and lift whatever curse it is that—

BO: Let me just say something real quick. (*Beat*) This is the exact kind of bullshit I am not going to take right now. If anyone is being given the short end of the stick, it's me, all right, because not only do I come from a family of misfit disaster people, but I also have to walk through the world, trying to mind my own business, but getting accosted every fourteen minutes by some prick like you for being a white guy. Nobody asked to be born and certainly nobody asked to be born into the life they're given, into this—this—shitty history, so tell me what you want me to do. You want me to go back in time and spank my great-great-grandparents? Or should I lynch myself? You people just need to say what it is you want me to do! I didn't enslave anybody! I didn't lynch anybody! I certainly didn't give your grandma any fucking blankets or burn down her fucking village! You don't know my life!

RIVER: Why are you screaming at me? My grandma? What are you even talking about?

BO: Aren't you Indian or something!?— Part Indian— / Native American?

RIVER: WHAT?! No I'm not Native American!

BO: Then why are you dressed like that? Why is your name River?!

RIVER *(Confused, spiraling)*: Uh—I!—Uh!—I'm a white?!—I!—Buh!—I!—Uh!—Oh my—you think this has to do with—this has nothing to do with being white?! This has to do with you being a bunch of assholes! Except for you Cassidy! You're not an asshole! I mean, thank God Franz can even have a semi-healthy relationship with someone around here!

RACHAEL: Excuse me? *(Beat)* What relationship?

RIVER: I mean, if it weren't for her, this man might have never found out his own father was dead!

(Beat.)

TONI: I thought the lawyers found you . . .

BO: Cassidy, you better explain what this woman is talking about—

CASSIDY: We're just friends on Facebook? / What is the big deal?

BO *(Wheeling around on Franz)*: WHAT DO YOU MEAN YOU'RE FRIENDS ON FACEBOOK!

RACHAEL: HOW LONG HAS THIS BEEN HAPPENING?!

CASSIDY: Just since Grandpa's funeral—why are you screaming / at me?!

RACHAEL: Because it is inappropriate for a thirteen year old to have a secret online relationship with her uncle!

RIVER: Really, / Rachael, is that necessary?

FRANZ: Hey, come on, you guys! It's not a / *relationship*—

BO: / Frank, you shut up! I'm going to deal with you in a second!

RACHAEL: Well, yes, River, sorry some of us can't be so hip and relaxed around child sex offenders!

RIVER: / What?

RACHAEL *(Snatching Cassidy's phone away)*: GIVE ME YOUR PHONE! / GIVE ME YOUR PHONE!

RIVER: *Child* sex—what? *(To Franz)* Child sex offender?

(Beat.)

FRANZ: Wait—

TONI: Is there some sort of confusion?

FRANZ: Toni, shut up! Shut up!

RIVER: What is she talking about?

FRANZ: That is not what happened! River, let me explain—

TONI: / Okay, Frank.

RIVER: Who are you talking about?

TONI: Who do you think we're talking about?

BO: / Toni—

RIVER: The girl he . . .

TONI: Raped, / yes?—

FRANZ: Can you stop!

TONI: Statutory is still rape, Bo!

    (To River) What did he tell you, sweetie?

FRANZ: / Toni, stop.

RIVER *(Small)*: She was sixteen—

FRANZ: Toni, please stop. It was not—it was consensual!

TONI: She was twelve and you got her pregnant for crying out loud!

(River gasps.)

Oh, you didn't know anything, did you?

FRANZ: She told me she was sixteen—

TONI: Frank, it doesn't matter—you were still a / grown man!

FRANZ: She told me she was older! I didn't know she was that young—

(Suddenly, River runs off into the dining room.
    Franz starts to go after her, but stops himself. He wheels around on Toni.)

Why did you do that!

TONI: Why didn't you?

FRANZ: It was ten years ago! How much more am I supposed to suffer, Toni?! How much am I supposed to suffer for things I did when I wasn't the real me! I wasn't me yet! I didn't feel like a grown man! I'm a different person now! Why won't you let me be different?

TONI: This isn't about you, Frank. It's about the truth. I didn't do anything but tell the truth.

RACHAEL (To Franz): AND YOU HAD NO BUSINESS CARRYING ON SOMETHING LIKE THIS WITH OUR CHILD BEHIND OUR BACKS!

TONI: Rachael, give it a rest! It was Facebook!

RACHAEL: No, Toni! I am sick of you undermining me! Now I am sorry that Derek left you and I'm sorry the child who you think of as a "fuckup" now wants nothing more to do with you and I'm sorry that for whatever reason you seem to be resentful or jealous of me because I'm not someone who raises fuckups—I raise winners!—but I am not going to sit here and let you tell me anything about anything having to do with my kids, when you've got these two monsters you've raised staring you in the face. So, you want some truth, Toni? Here you go! Here's your proof! You may have Bo too scared to tell you, but the answer is yes—you are a crappy mother and a poisonous person and a life ruiner—so why don't you give it a rest!

(Toni looks at Bo, betrayed.)

BO: Rachael?

RACHAEL: What, Bo? I'm not in this family anymore! I can say whatever the fuck I want!

(A silence, in which Toni just glowers at Rachael—like a long, deep, ocean of a silence that pours through the walls and fills up the entire space and takes forever to drain way, before . . .)

TONI: All right, Rachael . . . I'm sorry.

(*—suddenly, viciously, Toni grabs Rachael by the hair, which sends everyone into calamity only after a moment of being like, "Wait, is what I am watching really happening?!" By the time folks are mobilized, Toni is halfway to the front door. Rachael shouts, twists, screams, squeals— terrified—trips and stumbles the entire time she is being dragged. Meanwhile, Bo is on the way to save his wife—*)

BO: NO!

(*—and, without thinking, he grabs his sister by the arm and basically throws her across the room.*

Rhys sees this and immediately throws himself into the scuffle—)

RHYS: What are you doing?!

(*—grappling with Bo. Toni recovers, pulls herself up, starts shouting at Bo and trying to half pull Bo and Rhys apart, but also fighting off Rachael, who, by now, is getting her own licks in. Franz jumps in trying to pull people apart—*)

FRANZ: Hey! HEY! HEY! HEY!

(*—but he gets sort of dragged into the fight and starts sort of defending himself. There is the commotion of people screaming and fighting with each other.*

River, hearing all this, comes back into the room, joins in, trying to defend Franz, but also pulling people apart—)

RIVER: Stop! Stop! Stop hitting him!

(*It is pretty vicious and goes on for a substantial amount of time, everyone blurring the line between offense and defense, working their issues out on everyone else, tapping into whatever crazy lizard thing exists inside of us that comes out only when there's a brawl but then:*

A child's cry—confused and scared—pierces through the air from upstairs. Everyone sort of stops and looks up at the top of the stairs, remembering Ainsley, who comes slowly down the stairs, wailing. Over his head is a pointed white hood—an old pillow case with two eyeholes. Everyone watches him cry and cry, dead silent, mortified.

Blackout. Cicadas.)

2

The living room, a little while later.

There is no one present.

Then a bickering is heard coming from upstairs, before Ainsley comes running down the stairs and out the door. He is trailed by Rachael, suitcases in hand, trailed by Bo, who is trying hard to calm her down.

RACHAEL: Then we'll fly standby, Bo! I don't care! I will wait all night in the goddamn airport!

BO: Rachael, we've already rented the van!

RACHAEL: No, Bo, we're going home! We've had enough Southern History for a lifetime!

BO: We can't afford three last-minute plane tickets—

RACHAEL: Bo, let me tell you what I can't afford: being physically attacked in front of my children! Do you know how humiliating that was?

BO: Everyone knows Toni is crazy—

RACHAEL: Your entire family is crazy—your brother threw himself into a goddamned lake, he was so crazy! And, in fact, it's infectious! Your family makes me crazy! I have never fought anyone in my whole life! *And* I hate myself! I always hate myself around you people! I can hear myself becoming this . . . annoying, shrill, Chatty Cathy, catty . . . thing around these people and that is not me, Bo! That is not who I am and I know this! Why do they have this effect on me? I ask myself every time: How is it that they have the power to turn me into this thing? And now I know: It's fear. I am afraid around them because they are violent! They need violence and I don't have that— that need! I don't like violence! This obsession, this thirst, it's inconceivable to me—I mean, your youngest child just walked down those stairs in your father's hood—as if we needed more proof!—I mean—what are we supposed to do with that?

BO: Rachael, we don't have to do anything! You heard Cassidy, they didn't even know what that was!

RACHAEL: Yes and that is not okay, Bo! Because what they do know is how we responded, which was with horror! And how are we supposed to explain that? They look to us to tell them how to deal with things—

BO: Rachael—stop—we tell them the truth, okay? We just tell them we don't know.

RACHAEL: Don't know *what?*

BO: I think Toni and Frank might have been a little right after all—

RACHAEL: Right about *what?*

BO: Dad was . . . maybe he was a bit unevolved in his thinking sometimes—but he wasn't some redneck and I don't think—he wasn't social enough for this sort of thing . . . After Mom died, he was, like, a shut-in. You saw that funeral. There was no one there—I mean—honestly, after all this, I'm thinking maybe this stuff was just—just—

RACHAEL: Just *what*, Bo!?

BO: I mean, those things were antiques! They were valuable! Maybe he knew that! Maybe they were for—for—for the Bed and Breakfast?

RACHAEL: Oh, really? For the special Klan room? Or the lynching suite?!

BO: I meant like an investment or something! Or maybe it was here when he got here—just stuff he'd wound up with—stuff he didn't know what to do with. You cannot just make assumptions about him!

RACHAEL: Well, Bo, I think that is a bunch of crap, but, whatever the case, he didn't deal with it and now he's dead, so it's *our* problem—

(Rhys enters from upstairs. Bo and Rachael fall silent, guiltily. Beat.)

RHYS: Mom sent me to ask when Rachael will be gone so that you and Uncle Frank and her can talk.

RACHAEL: You can tell her I'm leaving right now. *(To Bo)* You've got ten minutes and then we're going to the airport.

BO: Rachael, we're not—

(Rachael exits with her suitcases in a huff. Bo and Rhys look at each other. It's intense.)

Tell your mother five minutes. *(Shouting up the stairs)* CASSIDY, LET'S GO!

(Bo exits out the door, just as Cassidy is rushing down the stairs. Seeing her, Rhys tries to flee.)

CASSIDY: Hey, wait, Rhys! I was . . . just looking for you.

RHYS: You were?

CASSIDY: Yeah. Uh, I want to give you something. But you have to keep it a secret. I don't want to get in trouble.

(Cassidy looks around furtively to be sure no one is watching before she hands him a couple of photographs that she's dug out of her pocket.)

RHYS: Where did you get these?!

CASSIDY: I'm kind of a klepto! And they were going to throw them away anyway and so I took some for myself and I didn't tell anyone. Anyway, I think you should have some, too.

RHYS: What am I supposed to do with these?

CASSIDY: I don't know. They're worth money. You can sell them. Or you can just . . . have them, I guess. To remember me? I don't know . . . I feel like we're never going to see each other again.

RHYS: We'll see each other again. In a few years, we'll be adults and we can, you know, we can be friends. We can see each other whenever we want.

BO *(From off)*: Cassidy!

CASSIDY: I'm coming! *(Beat)* I'm sorry for throwing you under the bus—I didn't know what to do.

RHYS: It's okay. I'm sorry.

CASSIDY: For what?

RHYS: For losing the photos, for hitting your dad . . . ?

CASSIDY: Oh, I don't care. *(Beat)* Can I have a hug?

RHYS: Sure.

(After a second, Cassidy and Rhys embrace. It's awkward at first, but melts into something real.
Toni enters at the top of the stairs, tries to conceal herself.)

CASSIDY: You do give good hugs.

(They disengage. Rhys looks at her. Cassidy grabs her bag and starts to leave.)

Bye, cousin.

RHYS: Bye, cousin.

CASSIDY: Bye, Aunt Toni.

(Cassidy exits. Rhys and Toni look at each other.)

RHYS *(Trying to exit up the stairs)*: He said five minutes.

TONI *(Stopping him)*: Rhys, I want to say something: You shouldn't have seen that. I'm sorry. I'm sorry this all happened—

RHYS: Did you wake up this morning and thank God for your fuckup?

TONI: You are not a fuckup. / You are not a loser!

RHYS: Mom! *(Beat)* Please get out of my way.

(Rhys exits up the stairs. Beat, in which Toni is alone before Bo enters.)

BO: Well, are you coming down?

TONI: I don't know yet.

BO: What do you mean you don't know yet?

TONI: I don't know yet. I kind of like standing here. *(Beat)* Where is Frank?

BO: I don't care. Listen, when I get back to New York, my lawyers are going to handle this—

(The door opens. It's Franz—soaking wet, again. In his hands, he carries a pile of wet paper pulp—the remains of the photo album—a mess. He comes to the center of the room and plops it down. Beat.)

FRANZ: That's all of them.

BO: Frank, why did you even bother?

FRANZ *(Angry)*: I wanted to fix something! I just wanted to come back!

(Beat.)

TONI: You know what I just realized? I've known both you idiots your whole entire lives—isn't that crazy? I remember holding both of you—Mama handing each of you over in the hospital and me looking down on these . . . helpless little things trying to figure out the world. Bo, you cried the whole time, but Frank you just stared. You seemed so peaceful—happy to be here. Remember, Bo? You must remember—

BO: Is there a point to all this?

TONI: Yes, because there's no one alive who's held me. Isn't that sad? There's no one left in this family—in this whole world—who could have told me about the whole me—the me before I became . . . this. Daddy was the last. And, think whatever you want about him now, but Daddy held me. He knew me—maybe more than I'll ever know me— and nothing anyone can say is ever going to make that love less real. All this life you live—what's it for if no one's there to tell you about it? To hold on to it and then give it back to you? To remind you of the things you forgot or never knew you even knew? I always thought that was what family was for. *(Beat)* But we don't seem to be on the same page, memory-wise. We can't seem to get our stories straight. And why is that? Or is family just a bunch of mismatched memories—stories you tell yourself when you need an excuse to explain how trapped you feel or broken or cheated? *(Beat)* I wonder what kind of story this weekend is going to be? Tell me, Bo. What story are you and Rachael going to go back and tell people? That this is the weekend I kicked her ass? Or that I was crazy and attacked her? That I ruined everything? And what about you, Frank? That you came to be forgiven and I denied you? *(Beat, after no response)* Well, I have a request. If anyone asks, I want you to tell them that this is the weekend your sister died.

BO: What are you talking about?

TONI: Because I need you to kill me. Put me out of my misery because I don't like myself in these stories—in whatever stories you're telling. All I really tried to do was love you. I promise. Maybe I don't know how—you know, maybe I never did—but I need to figure that out for myself, starting today. And you are the price. *(Beat)* So, if anyone asks, I'm going to tell them I had two brothers, who loved me and who took care of me and who were there for me when I needed them. And I just hope we never find ourselves wondering where a certain memory or feeling is coming from, because now we'll just have to make something up. Though maybe that's what you've wanted all along. If so, congratulations. *(Beat)* I'm going to say goodbye now, go finish packing with my son, get in my car, and drive away. By the time I come back down, I really hope that, out of respect, you will both be gone.

BO: Toni—

TONI: Goodbye.

(No one says anything, as Toni goes upstairs, leaving Franz and Bo, alone. There is a very long pause, as the cicadas chirp, and they look at each other. Beat. A horn honks.)

BO: Rachael.

FRANZ: Bo—for the record—Cassidy added me as a friend. I thought you had told her about me.

BO: We did. She saw the obituary. You weren't at the funeral. She had questions.

FRANZ: She put up some photos from it. It looked like a nice service. *(Beat, referring to the house)* What's going to happen here?

BO: I'm . . . going to deal with it.

FRANZ *(Skeptical):* You are?

BO *(A little irritated):* Yes! *(Catches himself, then softer)* Is everything all right between you and River?

FRANZ: Yeah. We're, uh, we're working it out.

BO: You're really camping out back? Are you sure you don't want to stay at a hotel? Let me pay for a room. Please—

FRANZ: No. This was all part of her plan.

BO: Okay.

(Horn honks, again.)

Well, keep in touch.

FRANZ: I'll try.

(Beat, before they shake hands. It seems like one or both of them wants to go in for the hug, but one or both of them can't tell if they really want it or if they feel like they should want it, so the handshake probably goes on for a lot longer than it should. Eventually Franz disengages and heads out through the kitchen. Alone, Bo sees the pile of paper pulp on the floor. He kneels down to pick through it. It's useless. He gets up and crosses to the door to exit but, before he knows it, he is sobbing. He sobs and sobs and sobs with his hand on the door, unable to open it. He is trying to pull himself together but the harder he tries the more he sobs. Suddenly the door flies open and it's Rachael, mid-shout.)

RACHAEL: Bo!

(She sees him there. She is startled. She immediately closes the door behind her and reaches for him, takes him into her arms.)

Oh, Bo! Bo! What happened? Honey, what happened?!

BO: I don't know. I don't know.

RACHAEL: What, Bo? Tell me.

BO: I don't know . . .

RACHAEL: Oh, Bo, shh . . .

BO: Why don't I know?

RACHAEL: Shh . . . Bo . . . *(Holds him for a while, then)* Come on, we have to go—let's go—

BO: I don't want . . . the kids . . . to see me crying . . .

RACHAEL: Oh, Bo, shhh . . . It's okay . . .

(Rachael starts leading Bo outside, just as:)

3

The cicadas? They just go on singing—singing loudly, sing-
ing incessantly—a long, enormously complicated, deeply lay-
ered, entirely improvised, ancient song, which is mostly about
the morning, but also about the evening and the day but also
the night and the sun but also the moon and about waking up
and flying around and what it is like to fly around and about
loving each other and hating each other and fucking each other
and hurting each other but also about trying to find each other
in order to hurt and/or fuck each other but also about falling
asleep and then waking up again and the quiet and the noise that
accompany each day and the sounds of each other's voices and
the occasional music but mostly about the noise and the grass
and the sky and the air and the water but also the water in the air
and the heat in the air and the dry in the air and the birds in the
sky and the birds on the grass and the birds on the branches and
always birds—birds always—but also the sap in the branches

and the sweetness of the sap in the branches of the trees but also the trees themselves on the grass and the grass on the dirt but also the dirt itself and how they miss the dirt and how they miss their homes in the dirt, the places where they came from, and the feeling of missing the thing you can never go back to and the mystery of the way one moves away from it and through the present and the mystery of the present and the mystery of the movement itself and the leaves on the branches and the birds in the leaves on the branches and the branches on the trees and the trees on the grass and the grass on the dirt and dying.

And we can't understand a word of it.

Meanwhile, lights immediately come up on the living room, some day—any day. A knocking is heard at the front door. Someone says, "Hello?" Beat. Then more knocking. But no one answers.

Sudden blackout and lights immediately come up on the living room, some day—any day—just as a part of the floor collapses beneath the sofa and one of the display tables. Everything on the table slides off in a waterfall of breakage.

Sudden blackout and lights immediately come up on the living room, some day—any day. Somewhere outside, giggles are heard. Someone is egging someone on. A rock comes flying through the window and shatters it.

Sudden blackout and lights immediately come up on the living room, some day—any day. A bookshelf collapses.

Sudden blackout and lights immediately come up on the living room. It's some day—any day. A rodent of some sort darts across the space quickly. Or maybe racoons are heard fighting over scraps in the kitchen.

Sudden blackout and lights immediately come up on the living room, some day—any day. There is a thunderstorm. Lightning flashes. Wind howls. A tree branch is either seen or heard crashing through another window.

Sudden blackout and lights immediately come up on the living room, some day—any day. A part of the ceiling collapses, bringing the dead chandelier down with it, but just before it can crash to the floor, the chandelier is caught by some sort of cord and swings like a pendulum.

Sudden blackout and lights immediately come up on the living room over and over again.

And, every time, it is some day—any day—tomorrow— thirteen years from now—twenty-six years from now. It is the future. It is the present. It is any present. It is the past—any past—now.

Time moving faster, pieces of the abandoned place starting to disappear—chunks of wood, the flooring, banister beams— cobwebs emerging and emerging.

One day, lights immediately come up on a stranger in the middle of the living room, taking notes on a clipboard. He inspects the room with a flashlight, takes a couple of pictures. Just before he leaves, he takes a look around, thinking, "Look at this place." He leaves.

In the blackout, there is silence.

END OF PLAY

(a lecture/play for a very young actor-playwright)

Production History

I Promise Never Again to Write Plays about Asians ... was presented at the 9th Annual PRELUDE Festival at the Martin E. Segal Theatre Center (Frank Hentschker, Executive Director and Director of Programs), the Graduate Center, CUNY, in New York, NY, on October 3, 2012. The curators were Helen Shaw, Caleb Hammons, and Frank Hentschker, and the producer was Rachel Silverman. The Actor-Playwright was performed by Max Posner.

ACTOR-PLAYWRIGHT: I promise never ever again to write plays about Asians.

Now that I have your attention, I'd like to introduce myself. My name is *[Actor-Playwright's name]* and, for those of you whom I don't know, I am a *[Actor-Playwright's location]*-based writer, originally from *[Actor-Playwright's hometown]*. I also work with/at *[Actor-Playwright's place of full-time employment]*. I'm also *[other miscellany having to do with Actor-Playwright's professional or personal identity]*, a member of *[place of membership for Actor-Playwright]*, and tonight, I guess I'm actually coming out to you as having been working in another capacity for the last few years—as Branden Jacobs-Jenkins, a conceptual playwright.

(Coughs. Coughs. Coughs.)

And I'm sick.

Anyway, so a confession: I have been a bit of a critical theory junkie since college—pretentious, I know, and I don't care—but, in the spring of my junior year at *[university from which Actor-Playwright has just graduated]*, I was one of two undergraduates fortunate enough to be allowed into a graduate-level media studies class with the renowned cultural critic Rey Chow. The other undergraduate was a close friend of mine, Joshua Bailey-Pittman, who had actually exposed me to Professor Chow's work when I was writing a theater studies paper on David Henry Hwang, and Josh lent me her book, *The Protestant Ethnic & the Spirit of Capitalism.*

Basically in this book—and just to be totally reductive for a moment—Chow talks about the "politics of ethnicity" in the context of increasing capitalist commodification, and focuses on how exactly consumers/audiences understand any text to be, quote-unquote "ethnic" in the first place. *Her* specific example is "Chinese" and she posits the question what makes a "Chinese" novel or movie or play actually "Chinese." Is it the author, the content, the marketing, or what exactly? And she's basically asking us to rethink how commodities like art or even like, you know, clothes articulate "ethnicness," by looking at the very processes that make that kind of articulation possible and, honestly, she's just interrogating uses of the idea of "ethnicity" itself as a kind of commodity. But, to take that model one step forward, if we think of ethnicity as a categorical set, including specific ethnicities such as black, or Jewish, or Chinese, or Mormon, that would actually posit four separate commodities and, in the capitalist system, not all commodities contain the same value. Thus how much is a Chinese ethnicity as a commodity valued next to a Native American ethnicity as a commodity? And, taking that model one step forward, in what are artistic claims of resistance by an ethnic group on the basis of their ethnicity complicit with the macro social structures that created the very category of ethnic subjects themselves, e.g., capitalism? And blah, blah, blah, blah, blah. Theory, theory, theory. I don't know if you followed any of that.

Anyway, it's amazing. She's amazing. I learned a lot and, in her course on "Performance and Media," we were given the option to either write a research paper for our final project or carry out a social experiment with an ethnographic component. Given my burgeoning interest in the theater at this time, Josh, who couldn't be here tonight as he is doing his master's in performance studies at Northwestern, and I, inspired by Rey Chow's book—and another text we read in class, *The Melancholy of Race* by Anne Cheng—thought it might be an interesting final project to fashion ethnic artistic personas—"playwrights"—whose artistic agendas were not about claims of "ethnic resistance" but instead about answering this question that Chow poses: In what ways are claims of resistance by an ethnic group complicit with the macro social structures that created the very category of ethnic subjects?—essentially, deconstructing this idea of ethnicity as a "commodity." We would write some fake, super-mediocre plays for them—which took like no one time—but sort of like contained "provocative" language and some stuff about stereotypes, and see how well they did in the literary market, and they did pretty well and one did extremely well, comparatively.

Initially there were three of these fake playwrights. The first was a Latinx playwright, which we abandoned rather early, given neither of us spoke the Spanish, and whose given name we have chosen not to reveal as some of her "work" might still be burning off in circulation. The second was Branden Jacobs-Jenkins, a quote-unquote "black" playwright with whom we've had the most quote-unquote "success," and for whom, as a result of this success, we've had to hire a young unknown actor out of Washington, DC, Malik Robinson, to play him for various public components of the project. The third was an

Asian playwright, whose given name we are also choosing
not to disclose as some of her work is still very much in
circulation, but tonight I am here to inform you, we will
be discontinuing the Asian component of our experiment.

The reason for this is simple: Asian plays, we've learned,
simply do not pay. We don't *totally* understand why this is,
but: "Asian plays? They no pay!" Or, at least, the deconstructivist "Asian" plays simply do not make money, in
our experiences. Why this is we do not know. We do not
know why people don't really care that much about deconstruction and being meta about Asian-ness. For whatever
reason, they don't seem to have the commercial appeal
of deconstructivist "black" plays. Which isn't to say that
regular Asian plays make any money either . . .

Take for instance the recent revelation by master playwright and Asian-American David Henry Hwang in the
New York Times, when it was reported that he earned
only $15,000 for three years of work on his Obie-winning
and Pulitzer-nominated play *Yellow Face*—an average
of $5000 a year. For a play that, in many ways, decon-
structs constructions of Asian-ness in the theater. (By
contrast, *Neighbors*, the non-Obie-winning play written
collaboratively by Joshua and myself under the name
"Branden Jacobs-Jenkins," deconstructing constructions
of blackness in the theater, netted us roughly $40,000
over the same amount of time.) Hwang also revealed
that he only earned $50,000 for four years of work on his
play *Chinglish*, which opened on Broadway to middling
reviews. This was not exactly a deconstruction of Asian-
ness in the same way, which may account for the spike in
its commercial value, but also, Yikes.

In comparison, in the same year, African-American
playwright Katori Hall's Olivier Award–winning play *The
Mountaintop* opened on Broadway to middling reviews,
recouped its investment and went on to become one of
the most produced plays of its decade, regionally. Also,

that same season, the number-one-most-produced play in America was *Good People*, by Caucasian playwright David Lindsay-Abaire, his first play to contain an African-American character. The number-two-most-produced play in the country was the Pulitzer– and Tony– and Olivier Award–winning *Clybourne Park*, by Caucasian playwright Bruce Norris—a *deconstruction of black-white race relations in America* and also his first play to use real-life black American actors onstage. Number three was *The Whipping Man*, by Latinx playwright Matthew Lopez, which is not about Latinxes but about Jewish black slaves.

Basically, "black" plays pay. Put a black person in your play and it will pay. And this is not just a present phenomenon but a historical one, stretching back as far as Shakespeare's *Othello*, Eugene O'Neill's play *Emperor Jones*, which attempted to formally deconstruct the black American psyche and which put O'Neill on the commercial map, right through Asian playwright Young Jean Lee's breakout success *The Shipment*, which attempted to formally deconstruct the black American psyche.

Honestly, I can't say why exactly the world is the way it is—why, for some reason, Asians just don't seem to make money in the theater. But, if you look at the last year in "theater news," Asians in the theater are a risky business. Take for instance, Mike Daisey, noted Caucasian monologist, who became the only news story about the theater that anyone besides "theater people" paid attention to, when it was revealed by Ira Glass that he lied about knowing a bunch of Asian people it turned out he did not know. Another example was the La Jolla Playhouse controversy which, really, no one but "theater people" cared about, but which was an important example. Duncan Sheik, noted Caucasian songwriter and one-hit pop wonder, and some other Caucasians, wrote a musical in which contemporary white people played a bunch of ancient Chinese people. What a risk! And why is this?

It might be simply because Asian audiences are just way more overly sensitive to their representation than black people. They get angry when you use yellowface, and, in general, Asians are also just angrier. They don't go to the theater ever, unless there are stars in it, and when they are in the audience they don't seem to know how to behave themselves—they bring in snacks, they don't turn off their cell phones and often answer them when they ring with their hip-hop ringtones. They also tend to talk back to the action that is happening onstage as if it were a movie and catcall when various handsome actors take off their shirts, etc. And then there are Asian actors. It is well known that Asians are amazing singers and dancers and musicians, but what exactly are you going to do with them in a non-musical? They also have language issues. They speak their own "version" of English that is not proper English and it is not pleasing to the ears, and at the end of the day, why make this difficult profession any harder than it already is?

How is it—when I'm on the train home to Crown Heights—that I can see *so many of them* and yet the theater has no interest in their stories!! I am angry. But it is not my job to be angry. My interests in this have and continue to be purely scientific, though the remarkable, though not particularly lush income, I receive through my work as Branden Jacobs-Jenkins is an added bonus, and the mark of a good scientist is knowing when an experiment has run its course.

So, in conclusion, we—Josh and myself—promise to you, our investors, never ever ever ever ever again to write plays about Asians.

(Beat, as blood begins to pour out of Actor-Playwright's mouth. This goes on for as long as it can.)

Thank you, everyone, for your time. Enjoy the rest of the evening.

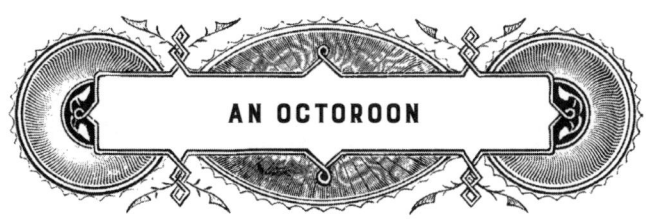

AN OCTOROON

An Octoroon received its world premiere at Soho Rep. (Sarah Benson, Artistic Director; Cynthia Flowers, Executive Director) in New York, NY, on April 23, 2014. It was directed by Sarah Benson. The scenic design was by Mimi Lien; the costume design was by Wade Laboissonniere; the lighting design was by Matt Frey; the sound design was by Matt Tierney; the songs, score, and musical direction were by César Alvarez; the projection design was by Jeff Sugg; the wig and makeup design were by Cookie Jordan; the prop design was by Noah Meese; the choreography was by David Neumann; the fight director was J. David Brimmer; and the production stage manager was Katrina Olson. The cast was:

BJJ/GEORGE/M'CLOSKY	Chris Myers
PLAYWRIGHT/WAHNOTEE/LAFOUCHE	Danny Wolohan
ASSISTANT/PETE/PAUL	Ben Horner
ZOE	Amber Gray
DORA	Zoë Winters, Mary Wiseman
MINNIE	Jocelyn Bioh
DIDO	Marsha Stephanie Blake
GRACE	Shyko Amos
CELLIST	Lester St. Louis

An Octoroon premiered at Theatre for a New Audience (Jeffrey Horowitz, Founding Artistic Director; Dorothy Ryan, Managing Director) at the Polonsky Shakespeare Center in Brooklyn, NY, on March 1, 2015, in association with Soho Rep. It was directed by Sarah Benson. The scenic design was by Mimi Lien; the costume design was by Wade Laboissonniere; the lighting design was by Matt Frey; the sound design was by Matt Tierney; the songs, score, and musical direction were by César Alvarez; the projection design was by Jeff Sugg; the wig and makeup design were by Cookie Jordan; the prop design was by Noah Meese; the choreography was by David Neumann; the fight director was J. David Brimmer; and the production stage manager was Amanda Spooner. The cast was:

BJJ/GEORGE/M'CLOSKY	Austin Smith
PLAYWRIGHT/WAHNOTEE/LAFOUCHE	Haynes Thigpen
ASSISTANT/PETE/PAUL	Ian Lassiter
ZOE	Amber Gray
DORA	Mary Wiseman
MINNIE	Maechi Aharanwa
DIDO	Pascale Armand
GRACE	Danielle Davenport
CELLIST	Lester St. Louis

An Octoroon received its European premiere at the Orange Tree Theatre (Paul Miller, Artistic Director; Sarah Nicholson, Executive Director) in Richmond, UK, on May 18, 2017. It was directed by Ned Bennett. The design was by Georgia Lowe; the costume supervisor was Holly Rose Henshaw; the lighting design was by Elliot Griggs; the sound design was by George Dennis; the composer was Theo Vidgen; the movement director was Ivan Blacstock; and the fight director was Kev McCurdy. The cast was:

BJJ/GEORGE/M'CLOSKY	Ken Nwosu
PLAYWRIGHT/WAHNOTEE/LAFOUCHE	Kevin Trainor
ASSISTANT/PETE/PAUL	Alistair Toovey
ZOE	Iola Evans
DORA	Celeste Dodwell
MINNIE	Vivian Oparah
DIDO	Emmanuella Cole
GRACE/BR'ER RABBIT	Cassie Clare
CELLIST	James Douglas

Dramatis Personae

BJJ	played by an actual playwright, an African-American actor, or a black actor
GEORGE	played by the same actor playing BJJ
M'CLOSKY	played by the same actor playing BJJ
PLAYWRIGHT	played by a white actor, or an actor who can pass as white
WAHNOTEE	played by the same actor playing Playwright
LAFOUCHE	played by the same actor playing Playwright
ASSISTANT	played by a Native American actor, a mixed-race actor, a South Asian actor, or an actor who can pass as Native American
PETE	played by the same actor playing Assistant
PAUL	played by the same actor playing Assistant
ZOE	played by an octoroon actress, a white actress, a quadroon actress, a biracial actress, a multiracial actress, or an actress of color who can pass as an octoroon
DORA	played by a white actress, or an actress who can pass as white
MINNIE	played by an African-American actress, a black actress, or an actress of color
DIDO	played by an African-American actress, a black actress, or an actress of color
GRACE	played by an African-American actress, a black actress, or an actress of color

BR'ER RABBIT   played by the actual playwright, or another
                artist involved in the production
CAPTAIN RATTS   probably played by the same actor playing
                Br'er Rabbit

The suggested cast size for this play is eight or nine actors.
Actor ethnicities listed in order of preference.

A Note on Overlapping

A slash (/) in a character's line denotes where the following character's line should begin.

A slash (/) at the beginning of a line denotes a complete overlap with the following character's line.

If such an imitation of human beings,
suffering from their fate, be well contrived
and executed in all its parts, the spectator
is led to feel a particular sympathy with the
artificial joys or sorrows of which he is the
witness. This condition of his mind is called
the theatrical illusion. The craft of
the drama is to produce it, and all its
concerns conduce to, and depend upon,
this attainment.

—DION BOUCICAULT,
"THE ART OF DRAMATIC COMPOSITION"

THE ART OF DRAMATIC COMPOSITION: A PROLOGUE

BJJ enters an empty, unfortunate-looking theater; mostly—if not completely—naked. He holds a remote control and surveys the audience for a moment, before speaking:

BJJ: Hi, everyone. I'm a "black playwright."

(Beat.)

What does that mean? I have no idea, but I'm here to tell
 you a story:
"Let's find a way to help you deal with your low-grade
 depression,"
my therapist recently said to me.
"Okay . . ."
"What makes you happy?"
"I don't know."

"Really? Nothing makes you happy?"

"Not really."

"What about work? Doesn't the theater make you happy?"

"I mean . . . Some of it. Not all of it."

"So you're not excited about your work?"

"I mean I'm not not excited."

"Do you have any career goals?"

"No . . ."

"Anyone's career you admire? Any professional role models?"

"In the theater?"

"Yeah—are there any playwrights who you admire?"

". . ."

"Anyone?"

"I don't know—"

"Just—just say the first name that comes to mind."

"Dion Boucicault?"

"Who is that?"

"He's a playwright. He's dead. He wrote in the nineteenth
  century."

"I've never heard of him."

"Yeah—no one cares about him anymore. He's dead."

". . . So your role model is someone no one cares about?"

"I mean, people cared about him when he was alive."

"Oh, okay . . . And what did he write?"

"Um, well, he's probably best known here for writing this
  play called *The Octoroon*?"

"*The 'Octoroon'*? What's an 'octoroon'?"

"It's a person who is one-eighth black."

"Ah . . . And you . . . like this play?"

"Yes."

"Okay . . . Well here's an idea:

Why don't you try adapting this *Octoroon*—for fun.

I think it's important to reconnect with things you feel or
  have felt positive feelings for."

So I did. Or I tried to.

But then all the white guys quit.

And then I couldn't find any more white guys to play any of the white-guy parts, because they all felt it was too "melodramatic."

I went back to my therapist and she was like,

"Do you think that maybe you're angry at white people?"

"Uh—what?"

"I said, 'Do you think that maybe you're angry at white people?'"

And I was like, "Uh, I don't think / so—"

"Like subconsciously?"

"Um. No. Like most of my best friends are white . . ."

Then my therapist was like, "Are you sure?"

"Yeah. I am literally surrounded by white people all the time."

"Are you really, really sure though? Like a hundred percent sure?"

I looked at my therapist, who was white.

(Beat.)

"Well, who needs white guys?" She said, nervously.

"Do you really need them? Why can't you just play the parts?"

"Me?"

"Yes. 'Color-blind casting'—that's a 'thing,' right?

And isn't that how the theater started for you? As an actor?

Maybe it's worth going back to the source of your relationship with this . . . thing you do."

"Okay . . ."

"So why don't you try playing the parts you need?

Maybe you'll learn something from it . . ."

"Like what?"

"I don't know. Whatever it is you learn from the theater.

Sympathy? Compassion? Understanding?"

(BJJ presses a button on his remote control and loud, crude, bass-heavy, hyper-masculine rap music plays.

BJJ retrieves a vanity table and folding chair from somewhere and starts setting up his makeup station, but then remembers something, pauses the music.)

Just kidding. I don't have a therapist. *(Un-pauses it, re-pauses it)* I can't afford one. *(Un-pauses it, re-pauses it)* You people are my therapy.

(BJJ un-pauses the music again and it plays as he finishes setting up his makeup station mirror, etc. Then he finds a bottle of wine or some other alcohol in a drawer, opens it, and chugs the entire thing. The alcohol has no visible effect on him now or ever. Then BJJ gets into whiteface—possibly tries to cover his entire body with it. This should go on for some time. After he is satisfied, he slowly turns around and, without taking his eyes off the audience, very, very slowly and very, very stoically gives himself a powerful wedgie. He takes the remote and turns the music down to underscoring. During the following, he continues getting into makeup, touching up, finessing.)

I believe an important part of being a good artist is recog-
    nizing your limits.
So I can respect the pussies who pussy out of a project.
I respect it when they get their "people" to be all like,
"Well, such-and-such doesn't really get the stuff about
    slaves."
I'm like, "What is there not to get? It's slavery.
And I'm not even asking you to play the slaves.
You're playing the goddamn slave owner."
I mean, God forbid you ask a black guy
to play some football-playing illiterate drug addict
magical negro Iraq vet with PTSD who's
secretly on the DL with HIV but who's

also trying to get out of a generic ghetto with his
pregnant obese girlfriend who has anger-management issues
from a history of sexual abuse—
in fact, everyone's been sexually abused
and it all climaxes with someone's mother having a
    monologue
where she's snotting out of her nose and crying everywhere
because she's been caught smoking crack
and fired from her job as a hotel maid . . .

(Beat.)

(I just made that up . . . Dibs.)

(Beat.)

God forbid any actor of color not jump at the chance
to play an offensive bag of garbage
so far from his own life
but which some idiot critic or marketing intern is going
    to describe as
a gritty, truthful portrayal of "the black experience
in America," but the minute you ask a white guy
to play a racist whose racism isn't
"complicated" by some monologue
where he's like,
"I don't mean to be racist!
It's just complicated!"
he doesn't return your phone calls?
Then my therapist was like,
"Don't you think you ought to not shit where you eat?"
    and I was like,
"Well, what happens if I shit where I starve?"

*(Playwright enters, also mostly—if not completely—naked,
and stands in the back and listens.)*

"Black playwright."
I can't even wipe my ass
without someone trying to accuse me
of deconstructing the race problem in America.
I even tried writing a play about
talking farm animals once—
just to avoid talking about people
and this artistic director was like, "Oh my God!
You're totally deconstructing African folktales, aren't you?"
I'm like,
"No. I'm just writing about farm animals."
And she's like,
"No, no. You're totally deconstructing the African folktales.
That's totally what you're doing."
And I was like, "Bitch!
I'm not fucking deconstructing
any fucking African fucking folktales!
I'm writing a fucking play about
my issues with substance abuse
and then I am attributing the dialogue to a
fucking fox
and a fucking rabbit
to protect identities! *Fuck you!*
Give me a fucking break!"
And, by "break," I mean a full-scale workshop production.

*(BJJ puts a blond wig on—the final touch. If the music hasn't
ended now, BJJ pauses it.)*

So then my therapist asked me about my dreams
and I told her about this dream I had recently.
A dream I keep having.
Basically, I am being attacked by a swarm of bees.
I am covered in bees. Bees are all over me—
all over my arms and legs, my chest
all over my neck, all over my face, in my eyes—

and I can't see a thing.
And, I don't know if you know this,
but the majority of deaths resulting from bee swarms
are not from bee stings
but actually from suffocation.
Basically, bees have evolved
to locate your breath and they follow it
to your face, where some of them
cover your eyes to blind you
and others climb inside your nostrils and mouth,
causing you to choke to death.
It's all very organized
in that terrifying way nature can often be.

(Beat.)

But, anyway,
in my dream, it occurs to me that I need to
figure out something to do
before the bees asphyxiate me.
And I start to panic. Every time.
And it occurs to me that
I should call for help, and so,
I start screaming. I'm like: "SOMEBODY!
HELP! HELP! HELP! HELP! HELP! HELP! HELP!
HELP! HELP! HELP! HELP! HELP! HELP! HELP!"

(Beat.)

And then, every time, I realize that I'm screaming.
And that, if I were actually suffocating,
I wouldn't be able to scream.

(Beat.)

So I must not be suffocating.

(Beat.)

The bees aren't suffocating me.

(Beat.)

And, every time, when I reach this exact point
where I realize this,
the bees dissipate. They fly away.
And the point of view changes
to that angle in your dreams
where you sometimes see yourself,
and I could see that
what looked like a swarm of bees attacking me
was actually a swarm of bees
that had come together
for a brief moment
into the shape of a me
being attacked by a swarm of bees
and it dawns on me, sadly, that
I wasn't being attacked by the bees.
I was the bees.
And when they dissipate and fly away,
they leave nothing behind.

(Beat.)

In other words, I was nothing.

(Beat.)

So my therapist goes,
"Well, you know, that's interesting because
the Ancient Greeks believed that
a swarm of bees was actually a sign that Dionysus was
    present!

You know Dionysus? The Greek God of—"
And I'm like,
"Yes, bitch, thank you! I know who Dionysus is!
I'm a playwright."

(Beat.)

(Into the mirror) A "black playwright."
Fuck you!
You're melodramatic!
PLAYWRIGHT *(Mocking him, slightly whiny)*: "You're melodramatic."

(Beat.)

(Off BJJ's glaring, again whiny) "Fuck you—meh meh meh—actors—wahh wahh wahh wahhh—waaaah—bees—waaaah—playwrighting—waaah—"

(BJJ glares at Playwright. Playwright glares back.)

BJJ: Anyway—
PLAYWRIGHT *(Still mocking)*: Anyway—
BJJ *(To Playwright, annoyed)*: Fuck you!
PLAYWRIGHT: Fuck you!
BJJ: No! Fuck you!
PLAYWRIGHT: No! Fuck you!
BJJ: Fuuuuuuuuuck yooooooou!
PLAYWRIGHT: Fuuuuuuuuck yoooooooou!

(The following is in complete unison:)

BJJ AND PLAYWRIGHT: Fuck you! Fuck you! Fuck you! Fuck you!
Fuck you! Fuck you! Fuck you! Fuck you!
Fuck me? Fuck you! Fuck me? Fuck you!
Fuck me? Fuck you! Fuck me? Fuck you!

Fuck me? Fuck you! Fuck me? Fuck you!
Fuck me? Fuck you! Fuck me? Fuck you!

(BJJ gives up. Beat. BJJ kicks over his chair and exits suddenly, leaving Playwright with the audience.)

PLAYWRIGHT: Where was I? *(Seeing the audience for the first time)* Hey, sluts.

(Throughout his speaking, Playwright very vividly and very intensely picks a mysterious wedgie that's been bothering him. He also seems to become progressively drunker, more belligerent.)

Feck, I'm drunk. How did I get so drunk? *(Referring to the folding chair)* What is this? *(Looks at it, picks it up, messes with it)* Is this a fecking chair? *(Remembers something)* Where is me assistant—me "intern"? WHERE THE FECK IS MY ASSISTANT INTERN?

(Assistant enters, an Indian actor—whatever that means to you—wearing a full Native American war bonnet and regular clothes. He carries on another vanity table and folding chair. He takes off the headdress and begins setting up makeup and costume for Playwright, at one table and makeup and costume for himself at another.)

There you are. Fix this!

(Playwright gives Assistant the chair to fix.)

What the feck is this filthy motherfecking place?
This isn't the Winter Garden!
What happened to the fecking Winter Garden?
I fecking managed the Winter Garden!
Our fecking toilets were nicer than this place.

There's not even a fecking petting zoo here.
Where's your petting zoo, huh?
(*Notices Assistant looking at him*) What? Why'd you look at me like dat?

(*Assistant whispers something in Playwright's ear.*)

Wha—? What do you mean, it burned down?

(*Assistant whispers; Playwright collapses.*)

No! No? No! No! No? NOOOOOOOOOOOOO!!!!

(*Assistant helps up Playwright, who is muttering and inconsolable.*)

No . . . No . . . My precious theater . . . no . . .

(*Assistant walks the weepy Playwright to one of the vanities, pours him into a chair, and sets up a music-playing device with some speakers. He puts on some old-timey popular music for Playwright. This seems to cheer him up a bit. Assistant goes back to his vanity and starts preparing his own makeup, wigs, and costumes for Pete/Paul. Meanwhile, Playwright clumsily begins to get ready, starting with redface.*)

You know what's so fecked up? Time.
Why, you ask? Well, first of all,
I'm apparently not famous anymore,
which sucks. You people don't even know who I am.
You got the fecking playwright sitting here—
a fecking world-class famous fecking playwright—
Right in your face—
Dion fecking Boucicault.
You bunch of perverts— Watching me get ready like this.
Can't even get a private fecking dressing room.

There was a time when I ran this town!
I was like the—I was like
The King of the Theater.
Everybody hated on me and they were sooo jealous
Just like they were hating on and being jealous of Jaysus
but unlike Jesus
nobody could mess with me!
I had the World Theater at my feet!
Hits everywhere! International hits!
Hits in London!
And America!
And London!
I invented things! I pioneered things!
Like copyrights! Yeah, that's right!
I brought you people copyrights!
And matinees! I invented matinees, bitches!
Look it up!
And everyone loves matinees now, don't you?
Admit it! You love matinees!
That's like five things—
Not to mention me many stage tricks!
HOW MANY THINGS DID YOU INVENT?

(Beat.)

That's what I thought.
I did all that crap for you and what did it get me?

(Beat.)

Every ten seconds you're reviving
some one a Shakespeare's bullshits.
He was a pedophile—you know that, right?
And a terrible father!

(Beat. Starts getting ready.)

Though one nice thing about the future is you can
actually use negroes in your plays now.
That's pretty great. You really save on makeup.
But can you believe you have to pay them?
So we could only afford three negresses.
My assistant here has to play the other negroes.
Though he was a more convincing negro
than the ones who came to audition . . .
(Shrug) But that's show business.

(Beat. More getting ready.)

'Course, you still can't find any indian actors—
Hey, where did all the indians go?
Though, I suppose it's okay.
I was always pretty good at this part . . .

(Beat. More getting ready.)

You know—
my name is actually derived from Dionysus.
You know who that is?
The god of harvest and beekeeping,
wine and theater—that's who!

(Beat. Finishes getting ready.)

Isn't that weird?
I always thought that was a little weird.

(Beat. Surveying the room.)

Perverts. *(To Assistant, referring to the music)* I'm sick of
this. Change it.

*(Playwright puts on the headdress—his final touch—as the
Assistant changes the song. Another song starts playing—*

*probably whatever's super popular on the radio right now,
though preferably loud, vulgar, bass-heavy, hyper-feminine,
and upbeat. Playwright perks up upon hearing it.)*

(To Assistant) What is this?
I like this.
Make it louder.
I said, make it louder!

(Assistant can't turn it up any louder.)

Louder, you genius!

*(Assistant finds the remote and puts it into the speakers. It
makes the entire room quake, which Playwright loves.*

*Playwright lip-synchs for a little bit before the lip-
synching turns into something else. Assistant hurries about,
clearing the space, and hands Playwright a tomahawk
before exiting. Playwright gets lost in the song. Playwright
dances. Playwright headbangs. Playwright fancy-dances.
Playwright stalks his prey before thrashing about with his
tomahawk. The trashing becomes a convulsing, the convulsing becomes a shaking, the shaking becomes the music, the
music becomes the play. The music ends just as Playwright/
Wahnotee stumbles off, in his full Indian regalia, sloshed
and swigging from a bottle, completely unaware of his sur-
roundings.)*

**[I'M JUST GOING TO SAY THIS RIGHT NOW
SO WE CAN GET IT OVER WITH:
I DON'T KNOW WHAT A REAL SLAVE SOUNDED LIKE.
AND NEITHER DO YOU.]**

ONE

The Plantation Terrebonne, in Louisiana. A branch of the Mississippi is seen winding through the estate. A low-built but extensive planter's dwelling, surrounded with a veranda.
    Or not. (There could just be cotton everywhere.)
    Dido and Minnie are discovered. Dido is sweeping laboriously. Minnie is just sort of lying around somewhere, fanning herself.

MINNIE *(Eventually)*: Do you need help or . . . ?
DIDO: Naw, girl, I got it.

    (Beat, while Dido sweeps.)

MINNIE: You know, if you sweep on a diagonal with lighter, faster strokes, it's a little more efficient.
DIDO: Girl, what are you talking about?
MINNIE: Your arms get less tired and you let the air pressure do the work. Here. Let me show you. *(Takes the broom and*

demonstrates) See? I learned it from Lucretia over in the hayloft before I got transferred to the house.

DIDO: And your arms feel less tired?

MINNIE: Yes, girl. And it takes the stress off your lower back. Here. *(Gives the broom back)* You want a banana?

DIDO: No! Do not get us in trouble!

MINNIE *(Taking a banana)*: It's just a banana. Relax! Shit, I picked 'em . . .

(Beat.)

(Eating) So what was working with Mammy like?

DIDO: The worst. I'm glad that old witch finally up and died. I already like you much better.

MINNIE: Yeeuh. I ain't never really knowed her, but she used to be taking care of me when I was little and she was mean as hell.

DIDO: Yeah she was.

MINNIE: She be taking care of you when you was little?

DIDO: I ain't growed up here.

MINNIE: You didn't?

DIDO: Naw, girl. I grew up at the Sunnyside place on the other side of the mountain. Massa Peyton won me in a poker game like ten years ago.

MINNIE: Ohhhhh. Okay. So you know Chris and Darnell and 'nem?

DIDO: Yeah. How you know Chris and Darnell, girl?

MINNIE: Oh, you know, Chris was messin' with Trisha over in the sugar mill for a li'l bit an' I met him and Darnell through her at a slave mixer over by the river before she dumped him because, you know, she couldn't deal with the long-distance.

DIDO: Okay, okay—

MINNIE: Yeeuh. So.

(Beat. Minnie sunbathes.)

Can you believe that Massa Peyton's been dead for two months?

DIDO: I know, right? Seem like only yesterday.

MINNIE: You really think Mrs. Peyton's upstairs dying from heartbreak?

DIDO: No. That bitch is dying cuz she's old as hell.

MINNIE: I know, right?

(Beat.)

You ever had to fuck him?

DIDO: Who?

MINNIE: Massa / Peyton.

DIDO: Oh, naw! You?

MINNIE: Naw, he only like light-skinnded girls. But Renee, you know, who was fuckin' him all the time, she said he had the biggest dick she ever seen?

DIDO: Really?

MINNIE: Yeeuh. Apparently that old-ass man was hung like a horse.

DIDO: That is gross.

MINNIE: I know, right? And now he dead.

(Beat.)

Whatchu think of the new Massa?

DIDO: Massa George?

MINNIE: Yeah.

DIDO: He a'ight. He don't seem to really know what he doin' just yet but he'll figure it out. Being a slavemaster ain't that hard.

MINNIE: Would you fuck him?

DIDO: No, Minnie! Damn! Would you?

(Beat. Minnie would.)

MINNIE: But I kind of get the feeling you don't really get a say in the matter.

(Beat.)

Damn it's hot!

(Grace, who is very pregnant, wanders in, carrying something heavy from one place to some other place. The women all look at each other. They clearly don't like each other.)

(Super-nice, super-fake) Hey, Grace!
GRACE: Hi . . .

(Grace exits. Minnie watches her leave then rolls her eyes.)

MINNIE: Ugh, I can't stand her. She is so fake.
DIDO: Right?

(Minnie goes back to sunbathing. Beat.)

MINNIE: Hey, Dido.
DIDO: Yeah?
MINNIE: You ever thought of running away?
DIDO: Aw, hell naw. What am I going to look like running through this hot-ass swamp? Uh-uh.
MINNIE: I know, right? Grace's ass always talking about running away now that Massa dead and I'm like, "Bitch, you need to calm your busybody ass down." Haven't she heard these slavecatchers got these new dogs nowadays that can fly and who are trained to fuckin' drag yo' ass out of trees and carry you back? And then, even if you can outsmart these flying dogs, once you free, what you gonna do once you free? You just gonna walk up in somebody house and be like, "Hey. I'm a slave. Help me." That kind of naivety

is how niggas get kilt. I ain't never met a white person in my life who try'na help you escape from slavery. Like, you know? Grace is such a mess.

DIDO: Grace always actin' like she too good for everything. And I don't know what people think they running away to. Ain't nothing out there but mo' swamp.

MINNIE: I know, right? Anyway, I'm about to have me another one of these bananas.

(Minnie goes to help herself to another banana, just as Pete enters.)

PETE: Hey.

DIDO AND MINNIE: Hey, Pete.

PETE: I see you finished fruit duty already, Minnie. Good job. You settling in alright?

MINNIE: Almost. I like the new servants' quarters but I think my room might be a little haunted—

(People are heard in the house coming outside. It's Dora and George. Upon hearing them, Pete transforms into some sort of folk figure. Dora and George enter. Dora looks distraught. George comforts her half-heartedly.)

PETE *(To Minnie, slapping her hand)*: Hey! Hey! Drop dat banana fo' I murdah you!

MINNIE *(Dropping the banana)*: Ow! What the hell?

GEORGE: What's, the matter, nigger Pete?

PETE: It's dis black—trash, new Mas'r George; dey's getting too numerous round and dis property needs clearin'! When I gets time, I'm gonna have to kill some of 'em fo' sure!

GEORGE: But weren't they all born on this estate?

PETE: Deez trashy darkies? Born here? What? On beautiful Terrebonne?! Don't believe it, Mas'r George—dem black tings never was born at all; dey growed up one mornin' frum da roots of a sassafras tree / in the swamp.

DIDO *(Exiting; to Minnie)*: He do this every morning. You'll get used to it.

PETE *(After Dido)*: Git out, you— Ya, ya!

(Pete sits down somewhere and eventually drifts off to sleep. Meanwhile, Minnie and Dora look at each other.)

DORA *(To Minnie)*: Well, don't just stand there. Fan me.

(Minnie begins to fan Dora.)

GEORGE: Ha ha ha— How I enjoy the folksy ways of the niggers down here. All the ones I've ever known were either filthy ape-like Africans of Paris or the flashy uppity darkies of New York. Here, though, the negro race is so quaint and vibrant and colorful—much like the landscape. And so full of wisdom and cheer and tall tales. I should write a book. Why, Pete was telling me a wonderful folktale, have you heard it? It's about a rabbit who wants to put on a show for the rest of the animals in the—

DORA *(Grief-stricken)*: George, I don't understand how you can be appreciating the folksy wisdom of the niggers with your dear aunt in the condition she is in! Why, she's nearly paralyzed with grief.

GEORGE: Yes, yes, Miss Sunnyside. I'm sorry. You're right. It's just that, in the few days since I've arrived from my beloved Paris, my senses have been so overstimulated by all the raw beauty of everything here, the wildness, the very essence of life—I can barely stay focused on the matters before me—

DORA *(Swept up, flirty)*: Dear George, what poetry you seem to have always at your disposal. When you speak, you sound just like your dear dead uncle—capable of such . . . *(Butchering the French)* joie de vivre amid this gloom. If you weren't as handsome and finely built as you are, I'd say you were his very ghost—his living ghost. *(To Minnie)* What are you doing? Stop fanning me!

(Minnie stops fanning.)

GEORGE: Well, I must admit my artistic pursuits have probably gifted me certain sensitivities . . .

DORA: Ah yes— From what I understand, you were living as an artiste en Paris? Ouais? *(Thinking she's saying something else)* Voo vay voo poo shay poopoo mwah.

GEORGE: Uh . . . well my late uncle did very generously fund my studies abroad in the fine arts. I thought I would make a living as a photographer, but I realize now it was probably no more than a pipe dream—

DORA: Hush. I'm sure that was no time wasted. *(Suggestively)* For I'd love to have my figure taken with your apparatus.

GEORGE: That could be arranged. You know, I have brought my camera with me. I've been trying to make some improvements on it, you see—I've invented a kind of self-developing liquid which when applied to the photographic plates—

DORA *(Interrupting)*: Shh, shh, shh. That's boy stuff; I'm a girl. *(Beat)* Oh, George! You are such a breath of fresh air! If only you had arrived here some years before your uncle died—things might have turned out differently! You might have foiled Mr. M'Closky's knavery . . .

GEORGE: Who is this M'Closky everyone speaks of with such disdain?

DORA: Oh, goodness, you do have much to learn. Thank God you've found me. M'Closky was your uncle's overseer before he died and is the man you have to thank for your family's misfortune.

GEORGE: How so?

DORA: Well, your dear uncle—rest his soul—was foolish with his money—and if he thought he knew gambling, that snake M'Closky certainly knew it better and, by the end of eight years, card game by card game and piece by piece, Jacob M'Closky has craftily found himself proprietor of the richest half of this estate. Now, because of him, you and your poor aunt upstairs have been run aground—

GEORGE: But the other half is free—

DORA: Yes. And yours, technically, but my daddy, Mr. Sunnyside, thinks that the property is so involved that even the strictest finances will scarcely recover it.

(Offstage, Zoe is heard singing.)

GEORGE *(Rapt)*: Is that Zoe?

DORA: Ugh, yes . . . Poor girl doesn't know she's tone deaf . . . *(Noticing her runny makeup)* Ugh, I've made such a mess of myself. Will you give me a moment? *(Touches up makeup, as Zoe sings. Then notices George, rapt, listening)* Do you like music? . . . *(Off George's nod, sultry)* Well, I'm a singer, too. *(Tries to match Zoe's singing—horribly. She gives up and Zoe's song ends)* I was told that you were seen riding with Zoe around the sugar crop?

GEORGE: Oh, she was showing me the property. What a bright thing she is!

DORA: Yeah, I guess? But she need not keep us waiting for breakfast, though. Pete, tell Miss Zoe that we are waiting.

PETE: Yes, missus. *(Screaming at Minnie)* Minnie! Why don't you run when you hear, you lazy critter?

(Minnie exits with a roll of her eyes.)

(To George) Dat's de laziest nigger on dis yere property. Don't do nuffin.

(Pete sits down on a bucket and immediately falls back asleep.)

DORA: That Zoe has been so spoiled by your aunt and uncle.

GEORGE: I've noticed all the neighbors treat her with condescension . . .

DORA *(Gossipy)*: Don't you know that she is the natural daughter of your uncle, and your aunt just adored anything her husband cared for; and this bastard girl, that another woman woulda hated, she loves as if she'd been her own child . . . and not a bastard . . . which she is. Zoe has had the education of a lady. I wonder what will become of her when Mrs. Peyton is gone . . .

(Beat.)

In any case, George, you should have called on me, darling, if you wanted an escort about the property. I live just over that mountain there. *(Shaking her ring finger in his face)* I know this place like the back of my pretty, lily white hand. Our families have been historically quite close, you know.

(Zoe enters, from the house.)

ZOE: Am I late?

DORA *(Rolling her eyes)*: Yes. Breakfast is waiting.

ZOE: Not if Old Pete is asleep. *(Kicks Pete)* Wake up you, silly nigger! Where's breakfast?

(Pete wakes with a start just as Dido enters with coffeepot, dishes, etc., crossing into the dining room. She and Pete make a big show out of attending to George, the new master.)

DIDO: Here it be, Missy Zoe! Dere's a dish of hoecakes—jess taste, Massa George—and here's fried bananas; jess smell 'em—

PETE: Hole yer tongue! Minnie, whar's de coffee?!

(Minnie enters with the coffee.)

MINNIE: He'ah, Massa Geor—

PETE *(Snatches the coffeepot from Minnie)*: Shut up! *(Pours coffee for George)* Dat right! Black as a nigger . . . You may drink dat, Mas'r George.

(George drinks it, loves it.)

GEORGE: Mmm!

DIDO: This a way, Massa George.

GEORGE *(Offering his arms)*: Ladies?

DORA: Oh, none for me—I never eat. You go on ahead, George. Zoe and I need a word.

(Minnie and Pete and George exit into the dining room. Just before Dido exits, Dora snatches a hoecake off of her plate and eats it hungrily.)

I find George so sweet. Is he in love with anybody?

ZOE: How can I tell?

DORA: Ask him, I want to know; but don't say I told you to. They say all the women in Paris were in love with him, which I feel I shall be. When he speaks to one he does it so easy, so gentle; it isn't barroom style; love lined with drinks, sighs tinged with tobacco.

(A cry is heard off, disturbing her reverie.)

What is that?

ZOE: It's Paul and his indian companion.

DORA: Ugh, why does Mrs. Peyton allow that pickaninny to run all over these swamps instead of hoeing cane like a proper slave?

ZOE: The child was a favorite of my father's. Mrs. Peyton couldn't bear to see him put to work.

(Enter Paul, being chased by M'Closky, who is trailed by Wahnotee.)

M'CLOSKY: See here, you imp! If I catch you and your redskin poaching in my swamps again, I'll cut me a switch and cane the black off of you!

PAUL: You cane me, Mas'r Clostry, but I guess you take a berry long stick to Wahnotee; he make bacon of you.

M'CLOSKY: Make bacon of me— You callin' me a pig?

(M'Closky grabs hold of Paul and seizes his whip. Wahnotee grabs M'Closky's arm, forcing him to drop the whip. M'Closky pulls out his knife as if to stab Wahnotee.)

ZOE: Oh, sir! Don't, pray, don't!

M'CLOSKY *(Hearing Zoe, putting away his knife)*: Darn you, redskin, I'll pay you off some day, both of ye!

DORA: That indian is a nuisance. Why don't he return to his nation out west?

M'CLOSKY: He's too fond of thieving and whiskey.

ZOE: Don't speak ill of poor Wahnotee! He is a gentle creature, and remains here because he loves that boy. When Paul was taken down with the fever, the indian sat outside the hut, and neither ate, slept, nor spoke till the child could call him to his bedside. He who can love so well is honest.

DORA: Whatever. *(To Wahnotee)* Go—back—to—your—people!

WAHNOTEE: Sleugh?

PAUL: He don't understand; he speaks a mash-up of indian, french, and mexican. Wahnotee Patira na sepau assa wigi-ran?

WAHNOTEE: Weal Omenee.

PAUL: Says he'll go if I'll go with him. He calls me Omenee, the Pigeon, and Miss Zoe is Ninemoosha, the Sweetheart.

WAHNOTEE *(Pointing to Zoe, obviously in love)*: Ninemoosha.

PAUL: Where is Mas'r George? We're goin' hunting!

DORA *(Aside to Zoe)*: Zoe, George can't go; I want him to stay and make love to me—that's what I came for!

ZOE: Paul, Mrs. Peyton is expecting a very important letter. Before you hunt with Massa Peyton, you must run over to the landing; the steamer from New Orleans passed up the river last night, and if there's any mail they have thrown it ashore.

PAUL: But I'm afraid to take Wahnotee to the shed! There's rum there!

WAHNOTEE: Rum?!

ZOE: Away with you, Paul. Bring the mailbag here.

PAUL: Come, then, but if I catch you drinkin', oh, laws-a-mussey, I'll gib it you! Now mind.

(Paul exits with Wahnotee.)

M'CLOSKY: I'm here to see Mrs. Peyton. Where is she?

DORA: Mrs. Peyton is feeling a bit under the weather, but her nephew, Mr. Peyton, is newly arrived from Paris, if you'd like to see him.

M'CLOSKY: This ain't a social call. I bring Mrs. Peyton news: her late husband's banker from New Orleans is dead, the executors are winding up his affairs, and have foreclosed on all overdue mortgages, so Terrebonne is for sale. Here's the paper with the advertisement.

(M'Closky presents the newspaper.)

ZOE: Terrebonne for sale?!

DORA: Terrebonne for sale?! And you, sir, will doubtless try to become its purchaser.

M'CLOSKY: Well, ma'am, I s'pose there's no law agin my bidding for it—

ZOE: Wait! There is hope yet! Mrs. Peyton was just telling me that the house of Mason Brothers in Liverpool failed some twenty years ago in my father's debt. They owed him over fifty thousand dollars. She has not found the entry in his accounts, but you two could doubtless help find it. Why, with principal and interest this debt has been more than doubled in twenty years! Mrs. Peyton received a notice two months ago that the firm has recovered itself and that some funds might be anticipated. I'll go find his papers.

(Zoe exits into the house.)

M'CLOSKY: They don't expect to recover any of this old debt in time, do they? It may be years yet before it will be paid off, if ever!

DORA: Well, if there's a chance of it, there's not a planter 'round here who wouldn't loan the Peytons the money to keep their name and blood amongst us. Now, if you'll excuse me, I must attend to Mr. Peyton, the new master of this estate.

(Dora exits into the house, haughtily.)

M'CLOSKY: Curse these old families—a snooty lot of dried-up aristocracy. Just because my grandfather wasn't some broken-down Virginia émigré, or a stingy old creole, I ain't fit to sit down to the same meat with them? It makes my blood so hot I hear my heart hiss! And the presence of these Peytons keeps alive the accusation against me that I ruined them. If I'm ever to clear my name and reputation, I must sweep them from this section of the country. Yet, if this money should come! Bah! There's no chance of it. And if they go, they'll take Zoe—she'll follow them. Damn that girl; she makes me quiver when I think of her.

(Zoe enters from the house with a folio of papers.)

ZOE *(Putting the folio down):* Here are the papers and accounts— Where did Dora—?

M'CLOSKY: Stop, Zoe—come here! How would you like to rule the house of the richest planter in Atchapalaga, eh? Or say the word, and I'll buy this old place, and you shall be mistress of Terrebonne.

ZOE: Oh, sir, do not speak so to me!

M'CLOSKY: Why not! Look here, these Peytons are broke. Leave 'em and jine me—I'm rich and I'll set you up grand, and we'll see these families and their white skins shrivel up with hate. What d'ye say?

ZOE: Let me pass! Oh, pray, let me go!

M'CLOSKY: What, you won't, won't ye? Come, Zoe, don't be a fool! I'd marry you if I could, but you know I can't; so just say what you want. I'll put back these Peytons in Terrebonne, and they shall know you done it; yes, they'll have you to thank for saving them from ruin.

ZOE: Let me pass!

(Dora reenters, calling for Zoe.)

DORA: Zoe!

(Beat, as Dora senses something's wrong.)

Zoe, you are needed inside. Mrs. Peyton calls for you.

(Zoe exits. Dora gives M'Closky a suspicious once-over before exiting.)

M'CLOSKY: Fair or foul, I'll have her!

(Opens folio) What's here—judgments? Yes, plenty of 'em—bills, accounts with the bank—what's this? "Judgment, forty thousand dollars, surely, that is the mortgage under which this estate is now advertised for sale."

(Takes up paper, examines it) Yes, "Thibodeaux against Peyton, 1838." Hold on!

(Takes up another paper, reads) "The free papers of my daughter Zoe, February 4th 1841." Why, Peyton, wasn't you smart enough to know that while a judgment stood against you it was a lien on your slaves? Zoe is the child you had with your quadroon slave, and you didn't free her before the judgment! If this is so, she's mine! Though this old Mason Brothers debt—that may cross me—if it only arrive too late— Hold on! This letter the old lady expects—that must be it—let me only head off that letter, and Terrebonne will be sold before they can save it. That boy and the indian have gone down to the landing for the postbags. They'll idle on the way as usual; my horse will take me across the swamp, and before they can reach the shed, I'll have snatched up them bags— Ha, ha!

(Calls off) Pete, you old turkey-buzzard, saddle my mare. If I sink every dollar I'm worth in her purchase, I'll own that octoroon!

(M'Closky stands with his hand extended toward the house. Music. An attempt at a tableau. He holds the tableau for a while before Dido walks in with a washing bucket and some laundry.)

DIDO *(Realizing she's walked in on something)*: Oops!
M'CLOSKY *(Startled)*: Wha-ah-ahh?!
DIDO *(Also startled)*: Lawd, Massa M'Closky, I'se sarry. Woo, lawd.

(Beat.)

(Smiling) Is you gonna be out here for a while, or . . . ?
M'CLOSKY: Oh, no. I was just about to leave.
DIDO: Okay . . .
M'CLOSKY *(Starting to exit)*: Uh, and would you mind taking these papers back inside when you get a moment?
DIDO: Yassuh.

(M'Closky looks at Dido for a second, as if trying to remember something, but gives up—frazzled as he is—and he exits. After a second, Minnie enters, looking for somebody.)

MINNIE *(Seeing Dido)*: Girl, have you seen Solon today?

DIDO: No, why?

MINNIE: I just rememba'd that nigga owes me four pieces of twine and some pig guts.

DIDO: Girl, you know you ain't never gonna see that twine and them pig guts again, for real.

MINNIE: What you mean?

DIDO: Minnie, you know Solon a trick-ass nigga. Remember what happened to Rebecca.

MINNIE: Wait. Light-skinned Rebecca?

DIDO: Yeah.

MINNIE: What Solon do to her?

DIDO: Well, she had a baby—

MINNIE: She did?

DIDO: Yes, girl. And this one time, Solon was like, "Girl, let me borrow your baby for a second?" And so Rebecca's dumb ass like gave him the baby and then that nigga turnt around and fucking sold the baby.

MINNIE: What?

DIDO: Yes, girl. Apparently Massa was about to sell Solon and Grace's baby, but then Solon switched Rebecca's baby out for they baby at the last minute and Massa didn't know the difference so he just sold Rebecca's dumb-ass baby.

MINNIE: Oh my God. That is so messed up.

DIDO: But then Rebecca got sold, too, so.

MINNIE: She did?

DIDO: Yes, girl. Two weeks ago. They tryin'a keep it on the DL, though, because they not tryin'a let folks know they broke.

MINNIE: No wonder I ain't seen her dumb ass around.

(Beat.)

(Suddenly angry) Uh-uh! Ain't no way I'mma let Solon cheat me out of my pig guts like that! *(Shouting)* Solon!

(Minnie exits angrily, looking for Solon. M'Closky reenters, stalks over to Dido.)

DIDO: Hi, Massa M'Cl–

(M'Closky strikes her violently.)

M'CLOSKY: And don't you ever fuckin' sneak up on me like that again, you nigger bitch!

(An actual tableau.)

TWO

The wharf. A camera on a stand. George, Dora, Zoe and Paul are discovered. Dora is posing for George, who is arranging his photographic apparatus. Paul looks on, hidden from the others by his mailbags. At some point Br'er Rabbit wanders through, unseen by the rest.

DORA *(Aside to Zoe)*: Zoe, the more I see of George Peyton the better I like him; but he is too modest—that is a very unattractive virtue in a man.

ZOE: I'm no judge.

DORA: Of course not, you little fool; no one ever made love to you.

GEORGE: Just turn your face a little this way— It's been a while since I've done a portrait. Look here.

DORA *(Angling her head)*: Like so?

GEORGE: That's right. Now don't move.

DORA *(Aside to Zoe)*: I mean, doesn't George know I am an heiress? My fortune would release this estate from debt.

ZOE: Oh!

GEORGE: Okay, I've got four plates ready, in case we miss the first shot. I've prepared them with the instantly self-developing liquid I invented. Now fix yourself. Are you ready?

DORA: Ready!

(Dora poses in a completely unsustainable way.)

GEORGE: One, two, three.

(George takes out his watch. Everyone freezes awkwardly. It's quiet except for a gull or two. Br'er Rabbit wanders in again, pauses, noticing the audience from afar, and wanders back out. Meanwhile, Dora's smile and pose melt into something so hideous it's hard to look at. It goes on for a while and then it's over. George pulls down the camera apron.)

(Mildly disgusted) Okay, that's enough.

PAUL: Why she looked like she was having a tooth pulled?

ZOE *(Sees Paul)*: What are you doing there, you rascal! Ain't you took them bags to the house yet?

PAUL: I'm gwine! I only come back to find Wahnotee. I lost him! *(To George)* Say, Mas'r George, take me in dat apparatus? You got four of dem dishes ready.

GEORGE: Get out, you cub! Do as Miss Zoe says.

PAUL: Gosh, wouldn't I like to hab my likeness took!

(Paul exits, running.)

GEORGE: Well, that has come out . . . clear, ain't it?

(George shows Dora the plate.)

DORA: Oh, beautiful! Look, Zoe. Don't you think this will make a lovely gift for a . . . certain gentleman?

ZOE *(Looking—it won't)*: Yes . . .

GEORGE: Will you ladies excuse me for a moment?

(George exits.)

DORA *(Looking at the photograph)*: I like this part—

ZOE: Were you saying something?

DORA: Oh, right! If George would only propose to marry me I would accept him, but he don't know that, and he will go on procrastinating in his slow European way, until it is too late!

ZOE: What's to be done?

DORA: You tell him.

ZOE: What?

DORA: Tease him about his shyness—I'm sure it's plain enough, for he has barely spoken two words to me since breakfast. Then joke 'round the subject, before speaking out.

(Pete enters, puffing.)

PETE: Mas'r George! Mas'r George!

DORA: What are you blowing about like a steamboat for?

PETE: You blow, Missus Dora, when I tole you: dere's a man from Noo Aleens just arriv'd at de house, and he's stuck up two papers on de gates dat say: "For sale—dis yer property,"—an' after he shown some other papers to Ole Missus Peyton, she burst out crying—den I yelled—den de chorus of little niggers dey set up hollerin'—den de livestock reared up and—den de hull plantation—

(George enters, buttoning up his pants.)

GEORGE: Pete, what's the matter?

DORA: You are needed at the house. The sheriff has taken possession of Terrebonne!

ZOE: Pete, did you pass Paul with the letter bag as you came here?

PETE: No, miss; but dat vagabond nebber take the straight road, he goes by de swamp.

(Pete exits.)

GEORGE: Come, ladies! I'll escort you back!

DORA: Actually, George, you escort Zoe here. I'll run ahead with Pete since I'm so good at receiving comp'ny. You and Zoe have some business to discuss, uh, regarding the estate.
(To Zoe, aside) Now's your time.

(Dora exits. George and Zoe are alone.)

GEORGE *(Seeing Zoe)*: Poor child! She must be so sad now, thinking she'll have nowhere to go.

ZOE *(Glancing at George)*: Poor fellow, he is poised to lose everything.

GEORGE: Zoe, with our ruin, you might be left without a home.

ZOE: O, no; think of yourself.

GEORGE: I can think of nothing but the image that remains face to face with me; so beautiful that I dare not express the feelings that have grown up so rapidly in my heart.

ZOE *(Aside)*: He means Dora.

GEORGE: If I dared to speak!

ZOE: That's just what you must do, and do it at once, or it will be too late.

GEORGE: Has my love been divined?

ZOE: It has been more than suspected.

GEORGE: Zoe, listen to me, then. I shall see this estate pass from me without a sigh, for it possesses no charm for me; the only estate I value is the heart of one true woman, and the slaves I'd have are her thoughts.

ZOE *(Truly swept up)*: George, your words take my breath away!

GEORGE: Zoe, your mirror must have told you that you are beautiful. Is your heart free?

ZOE *(Confused)*: Free? Of course it is—

GEORGE: We have known each other but a few days, but to me those days have been worth all the rest of my life. Zoe, you have suspected the feeling that now commands expression—you have seen that I love you.

ZOE: Me! You love me?

GEORGE: As your husband—under the shelter of your love— I could watch the storms of fortune pass by without a care—

ZOE: My love! *(Realizing, recoiling)* My love? George, you know not what you say! You? My . . . husband? Do you know what I am?

GEORGE: I know you are illegitimate, but love knows no prejudice. Has not my dear aunt forgotten it—she who had the most right to remember it?

ZOE *(Aside)*: Alas! He does not know! And will despise—spurn me when be learns who, what, he has so loved.

(To George) George, oh, forgive me! Yes, I love you—I did not know it until your words showed me what has been in my heart and now I know how unhappy—how very unhappy I am.

GEORGE: Zoe, what have I said to wound you?

ZOE: Nothing; but you must learn what I thought you already knew. George, you cannot marry me; the laws forbid it!

GEORGE: Forbid it?

ZOE: There is a gulf between us, as wide as your love—as deep as my despair. But, oh, say you will pity me! That you will not throw me from you like a poisonous thing!

GEORGE: Zoe, explain yourself—your language fills me with fear.

ZOE: George, do you see that hand you hold? Look at these fingers; do you see the nails are of a . . . bluish tinge?

GEORGE: Yes, near the quick there is a faint blue mark.

ZOE: Look in my eyes; is not the same color in the white?

GEORGE: It is their beauty.

ZOE: No! That—that is the dark, fatal mark of Cain. Of the blood that feeds my heart, one drop in eight is black— bright red as the rest may be, that one drop poisons all the rest; those seven bright drops give me love like yours—

hope like yours—ambition like yours—passions hung from life like dewdrops on morning flowers; but the one black drop gives me despair, for I'm an unclean thing— I'm an octoroon!

GEORGE: Zoe, this knowledge brings no revolt to my heart. I love you nonetheless. We can leave this country, and go far away where none can know.

ZOE: And your aunt, she who from infancy treated me with such fondness, she who, as you said, has most reason to spurn me, can she forget what I am? Will she gladly see you wedded to the child of her husband's slave? No! She would revolt from it as all but you would!

GEORGE: Zoe, must we immolate our lives on their prejudice?

ZOE: Yes, for I'd rather be black than ungrateful!

(Beat.)

Ah, George, my race has at least one virtue—it knows how to suffer . . .

GEORGE: Each word you utter makes my love sink deeper into my heart.

ZOE: And I remained here to induce you to offer that heart to Dora!

GEORGE: If you bid me do so I will obey you—

ZOE: But no, no! If you cannot be mine— Oh, let me not blush when I think of you!

(Zoe exits, running.)

GEORGE: Dearest Zoe!

(George exits after her.
Beat.
Br'er Rabbit wanders in again, pauses, notices the audience, and seems to inspect it from afar for a bit, before exiting.
M'Closky enters.)

176

M'CLOSKY: I arrived just too late, the boy had grabbed those mailbags just as I came up. But he-yo! He's coming this way, fighting with his injiun. The devil keeps him here to tempt me!

(M'Closky conceals himself just as Paul enters, wrestling with Wahnotee.)

PAUL: It ain't no use now: you got dat bottle of rum hid under your blanket—gib it up now—yar!

(Wrenches it from him) You nasty, lying injiun! It's no use you pretending to be sober; I ain't gwine to sit up wid you all night and you drunk. Hey, war's e'rybody gone? Dar's de 'paratus! Oh, gosh, if I could take a likeness! Let's have a peep.

(Looks at Wahnotee through camera) Oh, golly, Wahnotee! I see you!

(Wahnotee springs back with an expression of alarm.)

WAHNOTEE: *No tue Wahnotee!*

PAUL: Ha, ha! It ain't a gun, you ign'ant injiun! It can't hurt you! Stop, here's dem dishes—plates—dat's what he call 'em, all fix: I seen Mas'r George do it—tink I can take likeness—

WAHNOTEE: *No, carabine tue!*

PAUL: I must operate and take my own likeness too—how debbel I do dat? Can't be ober dar an' here too—I ain't twins. Ach! You look, you Wahnotee; you see dis rag heah? Well when I say go, den lift dis rag like dis, see! Den run to dat pine tree up dar and back ag'in, and den pull down de rag so, d'ye see?

WAHNOTEE *(Reluctant)*: Hugh!

PAUL: Den you hab glass ob rum.

WAHNOTEE: Rum?! Firewater?!

PAUL: Dat wakes him up. *(Throws mailbags down, sits on them)* Pret? Now—go.

(Wahnotee raises the apron and runs off.)

De time he gone just 'bout enough to cook dat dish plate.

(Paul sits for his picture. M'Closky appears.)

M'CLOSKY: Where are they? Ah, yonder goes the injiun! And yonder is the boy—now is my time! What's he doing; sleepin'? *(Advances)* He is sitting on my prize!
(Noticing the tomahawk) But the injiun's left his tomahawk! I'll clear that boy off of there—he'll never know what stunned him.

(M'Closky takes Wahnotee's tomahawk and steals to Paul.)

PAUL *(Through a frozen smile)*: Is dat the damn injiun creeping dar? I can't move or I'll spile myself.

(M'Closky strikes Paul on the head. Paul falls dead.
During the following, a large pool of blood begins to gather around Paul's head and M'Closky's feet.)

M'CLOSKY: The bags are mine! *(Opens the mailbags)* What's here? Sunnyside, Pointdexter, Peyton; here it is—Mason Brothers, sure enough!
(Opens the letter, reads, motionless) "Madam, we are instructed by the firm of . . . the balance will be paid in full, with interest . . . you may command immediate use of the whole amount at once if required." This awful letter would have saved all! But now I guess it will arrive too late. *(Hearing Wahnotee approach)* The injiun! He must not see me.

(M'Closky exits rapidly as Wahnotee runs on and pulls down the apron of the camera. He sees Paul, lying on the ground, speaks to him, thinks he is shamming sleep. He gesticulates

and jabbers, goes to him, moves him with his feet, then kneels down to rouse him. To his horror, Wahnotee finds him dead, expresses great grief. His eyes fall upon the camera. He rises with a savage growl. He seizes the tomahawk and smashes the camera to pieces. Then he goes to Paul, expresses further grief, sorrow, and fondness.

    Tableau. Br'er Rabbit wanders through it.)

THREE

An interior of the Peyton home. Dido and Minnie are discovered. Pete wanders in and out dropping off chairs, which Dido and Minnie set up downstage, parallel to the audience. They are silent for a while before:

MINNIE: Girl, is it just me or has it been really quiet?
DIDO: You know, I was just thinking the same thing.
MINNIE: Right?

(Beat.)

(As they work) Even all these white people are being really quiet. I wonder what's going on today. I couldn't read that sign out front, because I can't read.
DIDO: I can't read it, either. You know it's illegal for us to read.
MINNIE: Yeeuh, but I was hopin' you wuz one of them secret readin' niggas. You know, like Rhonda.
DIDO: Rhonda can read?!

MINNIE: Shh, girl! It's a secret.

(Beat.)

They didn't tell you why they got us settin' up all them chairs?

DIDO: Naw, but I'm assuming it must be a party.

MINNIE: Oooh, girl! You know I love a white-people party. *(Does a little dance)* Where the likka at, where the likka at—where the likka likka likka likka / likka at—

DIDO: Minnie!

MINNIE: You know they get too drunk to notice!

DIDO *(A little harsh)*: Can you stop actin' fieldhand for like a minute? You work in the house now! You gotta behave yo'self!
    (Off Minnie's reaction) I'm only telling you this for your own good. I don't want you to get hurt. You see what happened to Two-Fingered Tommy when he got caught stealing from the pantry. Now he only got one finger.

MINNIE: Speaking of, you seen Tommy yet? He was supposed to bring up the milk this morning.

DIDO: No, but I ain't seen Priscilla, neither, with the linens . . .

MINNIE: Well, I saw Priscilla's drunk ass last night. She probably hungover. She is such a mess.

DIDO: Where you see her?

MINNIE: She came by the servants' quarters last night for a drink and to say goodbye—

DIDO: Say goodbye for what?

MINNIE: I don't know. Maybe she got sold?

DIDO: They don't let you say goodbye when you get sold!

MINNIE: Then maybe she takin' a trip? I don't know.

DIDO: A trip to where, Minnie?! Slaves don't take trips!

(They both realize something's wrong. Beat, before they both exit quickly. Pete wanders in with more chairs, as George and LaFouche enter. LaFouche keeps scratching at his face.)

LAFOUCHE *(Annoyed)*: I must say that, in my fifteen years of experience as an auctioneer, this is by the far the most poorly organized estate I have ever come across—

GEORGE: Well, respectfully, sir, I've only been here about a week.

(Beat.)

(Watches LaFouche scratch) Um. Are you okay?

LAFOUCHE: Hm?

GEORGE: I notice you keep scratching your face.

LAFOUCHE: I hitched a ride here from New Orleans in an uncovered wagon, so I'm sunburned. Leave me alone. What is this one name scratched on the list of slaves here? Number forty-nine, Paul, a quadroon boy? A runaway, I assume? There's been an epidemic.

PETE: Excuse me, sar, but ain't no nigger ebber cut stick on Terrebonne. Dat boy's dead, for sure.

LAFOUCHE: Oh, was that the name of that poor little darkie who was killed by that redskin? That steamboat captain outside was just telling me he's got a set of deckhands that just loved that child and that if they ever see that Wahnotee fella, they'll lynch his copper carcass on sight.

GEORGE: What is Captain Ratts doing here? He's going to invest in swamps?

LAFOUCHE: No. He's here to buy a nigger.

(Pete perks up.)

GEORGE: Hush.

PETE: Eh! Wass dat?

GEORGE: Mr. LaFouche—maybe Mr. Ratts wants showing around the property. You're familiar enough with the place? Maybe we can convince him to invest in swamps.

LAFOUCHE: Certainly.

(LaFouche exits.)

PETE *(Aside)*: He said Cap'n Ratts want a nigger. Laws-a-mussey! What am goin' to come ob us!!!

GEORGE: Pete! Oh, Pete!

PETE: New Mas'r George, is it true? Are we to be sold?

GEORGE: I'm going to say somethin' to you that has been chokin' me for some time because there's no one else to tell and I know you'll excuse it because you're a nigger and don't fully understand complicated emotions—but my aunt! She's dying, Pete! She's dying! And she just called me to her side, grabbed at my sleeves and screamed, "Oh, let all go, but save the niggers! I speak not for my own sake, but for the poor people here—these niggers, who have been born here, they will be sold, divided, and taken away! Heaven has denied me children—so all the strings of my heart have grown around and amongst them, like the roots of an old tree." And, Pete, I can't deny this poor old woman her dying wish. I know now what I ought to do—I can't marry Zoe, though I love her—but Miss Dora is upstairs here and she is in love with me and her fortune would redeem a good part of this estate, so I am selling myself, so that the slaves shall be protected!

(Dora is seen, about to enter, but she freezes, overhearing the following, before she ducks out with excitement.)

If Miss Sunnyside will accept me as I am, Terrebonne shall be saved—

PETE *(Touched by George's speech)*: No, New Mas'r George! Nooooooo!

(Offstage, Dora is heard singing—the same song Zoe sang in the first act—but horribly.)

GEORGE: Go, Pete! Go! You must go and tell the others!

(Pete exits just as Dora enters, singing. She's still horrible.)

DORA: Poor Mrs. Peyton.

GEORGE: Miss Sunnyside—

DORA: Yes?

GEORGE: Uh, permit me to speak?

DORA: Oh, dear.

(Enter Zoe, who stops before she is seen.)

GEORGE *(Awkwardly, reluctantly)*: In a word, I have seen and admired you! And if you would pardon the abruptness of the question, do you think the sincere devotion of my life to yours would succeed?

DORA *(Aside)*: He has the strangest way of making love. European I suppose . . .

GEORGE: You are silent?

DORA: Mr. Peyton, I presume you have hesitated to make this avowal because you feared, in the present condition of affairs here, your object might be misconstrued, and that your attention was rather to my fortune than to myself.

(Beat. No response.)

I mean, you feared I might not give you credit for sincere and pure feelings. Well, you wrong me. I don't think you capable of anything else—

GEORGE: No, I hesitated because an attachment I had formed before I had the pleasure of seeing you had not altogether died out.

(Beat.)

DORA: One of those sirens of Paris, I presume. I shall endeavor not to be jealous of the past. But now that vagrant love is—faded?— Is it not?

GEORGE: Miss Sunnyside, I have not learned to lie.

DORA: Good gracious—who wants you to?

GEORGE: I do, but I can't. No, the love I speak of is not what you suppose—it is a passion that has grown up here since I arrived; but it is hopeless and must perish.

DORA: Here?! Since you arrived? Impossible: you have seen no one. Whom can you mean?

ZOE *(Advancing)*: Me.

GEORGE: Zoe!

DORA: You?

ZOE: Forgive him, Dora. You are right. He is incapable of any but sincere and pure feelings. You know you can't be jealous of a poor creature like me. He loves me—but what of that? If he caught the fever, were stung by a snake, or possessed of any other poisonous or unclean thing, you could pity, tend, and love him through it, and for your gentle care he would love you in return. Well, is he not thus afflicted now? He loves an octoroon.

GEORGE: Zoe, you break my heart!

DORA: At college they said I was a fool. Pretty—very pretty!— but a fool. I'm afraid they must be right. Am I missing something here? I don't get a word of all this.

ZOE: Dear Dora, try to understand it with your heart. You love George. I know it. And you deserve to be loved by him. And he will—he must. His love for me shall pass away. You heard him say it was hopeless. Oh, forgive him and me!

DORA *(Weeping)*: Oh, why did he speak to me at all then? You've made me cry and I hate you both!

(Dora exits just as LaFouche enters.)

LAFOUCHE: I'm sorry to intrude, but the business I came upon will excuse me.

ZOE: Perhaps I had better go.

LAFOUCHE: Well, as it concerns you, perhaps you better stay.

GEORGE: Concerns Zoe?

LAFOUCHE: The list of your slaves is incomplete, sir—it wants one.

GEORGE: The boy Paul—we know it.

LAFOUCHE: No, sir, you have omitted the octoroon girl, Zoe.

GEORGE: Zoe?!

ZOE: Me?!

LAFOUCHE *(Showing papers to Zoe)*: Pardon me, ma'am, but do you know these papers?

ZOE: Yes; they are my free papers; but they were in my father's secretary. How came they in your possession?

LAFOUCHE: Mr. M'Closky found them.

ZOE: Found them? He purloined them!

LAFOUCHE: At the time Mr. Peyton executed those free papers to his infant slave, a judgment stood recorded against him; while that was on record he had no right to do away with his property. That judgment still exists and under it and others this estate is sold today. Those free papers aren't worth the ink that's on 'em.

GEORGE: Zoe a slave! It is impossible! My uncle was negligent and doubtless forgot this small formality. But surely the creditors will not claim the gal?

LAFOUCHE: One of the principal mortgagees has made the demand.

ZOE: M'Closky!

GEORGE: It cannot be! It shall not be!

LAFOUCHE: It must be. The proceeds of this sale must cover the debts of the estate. Excuse me.

(LaFouche exits.)

GEORGE: Damn those Mason Brothers, why couldn't they send something by the last mail? Even a letter, promising something! Zoe, they shall not take you from us while I live!

ZOE: Don't be a fool; M'Closky would kill you, and then take me, just as soon as—

GEORGE: Stop—Dora Sunnyside! She'll buy you; that'll save you, if not the estate.

ZOE: Not after we've confessed to her that we love each other—

GEORGE: Right! Why did we do that?!

ZOE: Because it was the truth, and I had rather be a slave with a free soul than remain free with a slavish, deceitful heart.

GEORGE: Zoe!

ZOE: Do not weep, dear George. Be a man. You now see what a miserable thing I am. Leave me now. I would be alone a little while.

(George exits, weeping.)

A slave! A slave! Is this a dream—for my brain reels with the blow? Sold! And M'Closky, my master—oh!

(Falls on her knees, face in her hands) No—no master but one. George—George— So like my father! Oh my father! My dear, dear father! Have I slept upon the benefits I received, and never saw, never felt, never knew that I was ungrateful? Let me be sold then, that I may free your name and give you back the liberty you bestowed upon me; for I can never repay the love you bore your poor octoroon child. Forgive her. You made her life too happy, and now these tears will flow. Let me bide them till I teach my heart. Oh, my—my heart! Hush—they come for me! Save me! No.

(Looks off toward a commotion) 'Tis Pete and the servants—they come this way.

(Zoe exits with a low, wailing, suffocating cry, just as Pete, Minnie, Dido and pregnant Grace enter.)

PETE: Come yer now! Stand 'round! I've got to talk to you house darkies—Grace, you might as well hear dis, too.

MINNIE: Pete—!

PETE: Don't make no noise, de sick missus har us! My colored ladies, dar's mighty bad news gone 'round—

MINNIE: Pete—

PETE: Shut up! Dis yer prop'ty to be sold—old Terrebonne—
whar we all been raised—dey's gwine to take it away—

DIDO: But Pete—

PETE: Hold quiet, you trash o' niggers! And dis ain't all. Now
listen—we tought datde niggers would always belong to
de ole missus, and if she lost Terrebonne, we must live
dere and simply hire ourselves out so we could bring our
wages to her—

MINNIE: Seriously, Pete . . .

PETE: Hush! But I tell ye, 'tain't so—we've got to be sold—

DIDO *(To Minnie)*: That's what's going on.

PETE: Will you hush! Now, I listen dar jess now to Mas'r
George— You shoulda seen dem big tears in his eyes.
He say de missus say, "'Tain't for de land I keer, but for
dem poor niggers—dey'll be sold." "But no," says he. "I'd
rather sell myself fust; de niggers—dey shan't suffer."
(Getting emotional) Yes, for you, for me, dem white folks
cried. Dey cried! Fo' us! Fo' us sorry, no-good-nothin' niggas! Now, I say, as dat ole man was always so good to us
and dat ole woman—for de pride of de family, let every
darkie do his best for dey sake—so dem strangers from
Nawleens shall say, "Dem's happy darkies, dem's a fine set
of niggers!" and buy us right up and together we'll serve
these fine white people! And everyone say, when he's sold,
"Lor' bless dis yer family I'm gwine out of, and pray send
me to as good a home!"

*(Beat. The women all look at each other. Minnie tries to
start a slow clap.)*

GRACE: What the hell is wrong witchu?! Don't you know everybody done run away?!

PETE: WHAT?!

DIDO: That's what we been tryin'a tell yo' black ass for the last
ten minutes.

PETE: What you mean, they done run away? Why didn't somebody tell me?

MINNIE: Ain't nobody told us, neither, nigga! Obviously.

PETE: But Grace—you still here—I thought you wuz head of
the Runaway Plannin' Committee with Solon.

GRACE: I was.

PETE: Well, what happened?

GRACE: I overslept, nigga. Shit. Mind yo' own business.

PETE: Aw, dis is da worst! Dis is da worst! *(To Grace)* How did
this happen?

GRACE: Eber since sweet little Paul was kilt, folks figguh'd
things was taking a turn for da worse, so Solon thought
it was time to take off while all these white people wuz
distracted with they personal and financial drama.

PETE: Laws-a-mussey! Get out of my way! I need to get tell a
white man what's going on!

*(Pete exits, running. Beat, during which the women look at
each other.)*

MINNIE: Well, at least this explains what all them people was
doing walking around.

DIDO: You overslept?

GRACE: Yes, bitch. I'm pregnant. I'm allowed to oversleep sometimes. Shit.

DIDO: Okay, where did the attitude just come from?

MINNIE: Solon couldn't wake you up?

(Beat. Grace starts crying softly. Minnie goes to comfort her.)

Oh, girl, what's wrong?

GRACE: I think Solon left me.

MINNIE: Whaaat?

GRACE: I think he ran off wit dumb-ass Rebecca!

MINNIE: Light-skinned Rebecca?

GRACE: Yes.

DIDO: I thought Rebecca got sold.

GRACE: No. Rebecca baby got sold.

DIDO: No, I thought Rebecca got sold last week to the Duponts.

GRACE: No, girl, that was Lucretia from the hayloft.

MINNIE: Lucretia got sold?!

GRACE: Yes.

MINNIE: Damn. There are too many niggas coming and going around here—I can barely keep track.

GRACE: Ain't no need to keep track no mo' . . .

MINNIE: Why not?

DIDO: Because everybody except us ran away, stupid!

MINNIE: Oh, yeah.

DIDO: And now we're about to get sold!

MINNIE: Oh, yeah!

DIDO: This is about the worst damn day of my life! It's even worse than the first time I got sold!

MINNIE: Yeah, I didn't wake up thinkin' this was where my day was gonna go. I can't believe nobody told us they was running away. Why didn't they tell us, Grace?

DIDO: Yeah. You would know.

GRACE: You house niggas.

DIDO: What?

GRACE: You house niggas. Y'all was livin' it up in the damn house all the time, serving everybody pancakes and shit while we wuz in the fields all day hoeing cane and picking a fuck ton of cotton in the hot-ass sun . . . So we figured y'all probably didn't need to run away.

DIDO: Well you still coulda asked us. That would have been the polite thing to do 'steada acting like a bunch of selfish fieldhands.

GRACE: And nobody likes y'all!

DIDO: Excuse me?

GRACE: There, I said it. Everyone thinks you're a bitch, Dido. And everyone finds the way you act kinda ghetto, Minnie. It's embarrassing to the community.

MINNIE: What?! WHO GHETTO?!

(Minnie rushes at Grace. Grace rushes at Minnie.)

DIDO *(Breaking it up)*: Hey! Hey! HEY!

MINNIE: She lucky she pregnant!

DIDO: There no use fighting about it now!

(The women cool off.)

GRACE: You right. You right.

DIDO: So Solon took y'all baby, too?

GRACE: What are you talking about? The baby is in my belly?

MINNIE: No, girl, your other baby!

GRACE *(Genuinely upset)*: Oh, shit, where is my other baby?!

(Grace exits, running.)

MINNIE: Girl, what are we gonna do?

DIDO: I don't know. I kind of liked it here.

MINNIE: Me, too. I feel bad for da Peytons.

DIDO: Why?

MINNIE: I don't know. They were some cool-ass white people.
I mean, they didn't never really beat us, you know? It coulda
been worse.

DIDO: Yeah. I heard on the M'Closky plantation they actually,
like, whips the slaves. With, like, a whip.

MINNIE: Whaaat?

DIDO: I know, right?

MINNIE: I am not trying to get bought by Massa M'Closky!

DIDO: Well, I saw him in that group of white men walking around
inspecting things.

MINNIE: Oh no! *(Remembers something, whispering)* Wait, girl!
You know who else I saw in that group?

DIDO: Who?

MINNIE: That fine-ass white man who own that steamboat.
With the tan? I think his name is like Rat or sum'n. Ratts?

Ratty? Rabbit? Ratface? I don't know. We gotta get bought by him, girl! Imagine: If we lived on a steamboat, coasting up and down the river, looking fly, wind whipping at our hair and our slave tunics and shit, and we surrounded by all these fine, muscly boat niggas who ain't been wit a woman in years?

DIDO: I don't know, Minnie, that sounds kinda dangerous . . .

MINNIE: Girl, come on. You yourself said you was tired of being in this damn swamp all the time. And I been on this plantation my entire life. I'm tired of all this dirt and dust and nasty-ass table-scrap food. Girl, don't you know on a boat they be eating fresh fish and skrimps and stuff? None of these fattening pig guts. Come on, girl, this is our chance to see the world!

DIDO: See the world? What world?

MINNIE: Girl, come on! I gotta idea!

(Dido and Minnie exit and, after a beat, Captain Ratts, the steamboat captain, enters from the audience, looking for special seating, on account of his obesity. Perhaps he picks a fight with an audience member, whom he accuses of sitting in his seat. At some point, LaFouche has to enter, and directs Ratts toward the row of seats Dido and Minnie have just set up. George and M'Closky, both played by BJJ, enter and join him. Time has passed and we are now at the auction. There is either one or ninety-nine people playing various bidders. Or maybe there's some clever way to force the audience into doing this.

Really all we need is one person to play Ratts. But I guess I worry about the whole thing becoming too Brechtian. Though, does it matter? Also, can I help it? Or maybe it's just whoever's been playing music this whole time? Or maybe it's just me? Maybe I sit in the audience of every show and play Ratts. Or maybe it's Br'er Rabbit? Let's just say it's Br'er Rabbit.)

LAFOUCHE: Well, I guess this is everyone that's going to show up. Captain Ratts, there's a seat down here in the front row. Don't be shy.

(Ratts takes his seat.)

Thank you, Captain.

(Fast auction-speak) Gentlemen, we shall proceed to business. It ain't necessary for me to dilate, describe or enumerate. Terrebonne is known to you as one of the richest bits of sile in Louisiana. So, gentlemen, as life is short, we'll start right off. Now, I'm proud to submit to you the finest lot of fieldhands and house servants that was ever offered. Send in the niggers!

(Pete, Grace, Minnie and Dido all shuffle in awkwardly. Pete is grinning a lot and wearing shackles for no real reason. Minnie and Dido are wearing remarkably sexier and more revealing slave tunics and have their hair and makeup done up accordingly. They spot Ratts and make a lot of suggestive faces and gestures in his direction. LaFouche is confused.)

Where are the rest of the niggers?

(Pete and George share a look, before George, embarrassed, rushes up to whisper something into LaFouche's ear.)

What?! What do you mean they've all run away?

(Commotion from the crowd, which may just be Ratts.)

PETE *(Gesturing to himself and the other slaves)*: Ah-ah-ahem. Hello?
RATTS: Now wait a minute— Why did you all remain?
MINNIE: Nobody told us.

(More commotion from the crowd, or just Ratts.
LaFouche bangs the gavel.)

LAFOUCHE: Listen, we're going to proceed because I've got two more auctions today and I have to be back in New Orleans by five, so let's start with . . . *(Going through his notes)* Number . . . *(Giving up)* Pete, a house servant.

PETE: Dat's me—yer, I'm comin'—stand around dar.

(Pete tumbles upon the table.)

LAFOUCHE: Aged . . . seventy . . . two?

PETE: Fo'ty-six, sar.

LAFOUCHE: And lame.

PETE: But dat don't mean nuthin'! Look ye here!

(Pete starts to sing a very unimpressive, folksier version of whatever song Zoe and Dora sang earlier, before he gives up.)

You know what? I'm tired of being a slave.

LAFOUCHE: What?!

PETE: Psych! *(Addressing the crowd)* What do you say, gentlemen? Shall we start the bidding at a million?

LAFOUCHE *(Annoyed, stopping him)*: One hundred dollars! Do I hear one hundred dollars?

GEORGE: One hundred.

PETE: Mas'r George—ah, no, sar—don't buy me—keep your money for some other that is to be sold!

LAFOUCHE: One hundred bid—it's a good price. He's yours, Mr. George Peyton. *(To Dido)* Okay. What's your name, little wench?

DIDO: Dido.

LAFOUCHE: We'll start with Dido.

MINNIE: Wait! Actually . . .

(Minnie goes over and whispers something in LaFouche's ear.)

LAFOUCHE *(To George, incredulous)*: The property is requesting that it be sold along with another piece of property? *(Off George's shrug, with a sigh)* You know what? This is a shitshow. Let's just get this over with. *(Back out)* So, Dido here, will be sold along with . . . ?

MINNIE: Minerva. Minnie.

LAFOUCHE: With Minerva.

(Minnie and Dido mount the table and sort of stare at Ratts a lot, who seems to respond. Over the following, they somehow manage to seduce Ratts into buying them.)

MINNIE: Heeeeeeeeeeey.

LAFOUCHE: Shall we start the bidding at one thousand for the pair? One thousand. Can I get fifteen hundred? Fifteen. Two thousand? Two thousand, to Captain Ratts. Can I get three thousand? Three thousand? Three thousand to you, Mr. M'Closky.

RATTS: Come on now! I really need some niggers! Please let me get what I came here for! Five thousand!

LAFOUCHE: Five thousand bid from Captain Ratts. Six? Six? Do I hear six? No. Five thousand bid from Captain Ratts. Going, going, gone. They're yours.

MINNIE: Yaaaaaaay!

(Minnie and Dido dismount and go over to stand behind Ratts.)

LAFOUCHE: What a steal. Next up is . . . a pregnant female fieldhand . . . with other child. A fertile bargain. Three for the price of one . . .

(Grace gets on the table holding her baby, which is, ideally, a white baby in blackface.)

GRACE *(To Ratts)*: Buy me, Massa Ratts, do buy me, sar.

RATTS: And what in thunder would I do with you and those devils on board my boat?

GRACE: Wash, sar—cook, sar—anything.

LAFOUCHE: Come now, Captain. Don't separate this poor heifer from her little niglets.

RATTS *(With a sign)*: Fine. Eight hundred.

LAFOUCHE: Eight hundred. Do I heard nine? Nine. Nine hundred to Mr. M'Closky. One thousand. One thousand to Cap'n Ratts. Do I hear eleven? Eleven? Eleven? Eleven to M'Closky.

RATTS: I'm broke, dear—I'm sorry.

LAFOUCHE: All right. Eleven hundred to M'Closky—going—going—sold!

(LaFouche bangs his gavel.)

MINNIE *(Trying to start something)*: Who ghetto now, bitch?!

(Commotion. LaFouche bangs his gavel.)

LAFOUCHE: Settle down! Settle down! *(To George)* I guess on to the property. *(Seeing Zoe hiding offstage)* Actually, wait, no, I almost forgot: the octoroon girl, Zoe! Thank God.

(Zoe enters, very pale, and stands on the table. Hitherto, M'Closky has taken no real interest in the sale. Now he perks up.)

GEORGE *(Rising)*: Gentlemen, we are all acquainted with the circumstances of Miss Zoe's position, and I feel sure that no one here will oppose the family which desires to redeem the child of your esteemed and noble friend and my uncle, the late Judge Peyton.

RATTS: Hear, hear!

LAFOUCHE: While the proceeds of this sale obviously promise to realize far far less than the debts upon it, it is my duty to

prevent any collusion for the depreciation of the property.
What is offered for Zoe?

GEORGE: One thousand dollars.

M'CLOSKY: Two thousand.

GEORGE: Three thousand.

M'CLOSKY: Five thousand.

GEORGE: Demon! Seven!

M'CLOSKY: Eight.

GEORGE: Nine.

M'CLOSKY: Ten. It's no use, squire.

RATTS: Jacob M'Closky, you shan't have that girl. Now, take care what you do. Twelve thousand.

M'CLOSKY: Shan't I! Fifteen thousand. Beat that any of ye.

LAFOUCHE: Fifteen thousand bid for the octoroon.

(Dora enters.)

DORA: Twenty thousand!

M'CLOSKY: Twenty-five thousand.

GEORGE: Yelping hound—take that.

(George rushes M'Closky/himself, who draws his knife. They scuffle elaborately—perhaps ridiculously—the actor literally wrestling with himself. The crowd reacts accordingly—the melee going on for a long while until George manages to disarm M'Closky and seems prepared to cut his throat.)

LAFOUCHE: Hold on! Stand back!

(Beat, as the fighting stops.)

This is your own house and we are under your uncle's roof; but recollect yourself. And ain't we forgetting there's a lady present?

(George/M'Closky disengage. The knife disappears.)

If we can't behave like Christians, let's try and act like gentlemen. I believe none of us have two feelings about the conduct of this man; but he has the law on his side. We may regret it, but we must respect it. Mr. M'Closky has bid twenty-five thousand dollars for the octoroon. Is there any other bid? For the first time, twenty-five thousand—last time!

(Brings gavel down) To Jacob M'Closky, the octoroon girl, Zoe, twenty-five thousand dollars.

(M'Closky jumps up on his chair, throws money in the air, and makes it rain—perhaps literally, perhaps figuratively—the theater is a space of infinite possibility.
Tableau.)

FOUR

The empty, unfortunate-looking theater, again.
BJJ and Playwright step forward from the tableau. Dark-
ness falls. Eventually, they are joined by Assistant, who is pres-
ently busy ushering actors offstage, cleaning up, checking email,
etc.

BJJ: So I think I fucked up. I had this really amazing concept
   for how this would all work with my limited resources and
   then—
PLAYWRIGHT: I grossly underestimated the amount of white
   men I actually would need here—
BJJ: especially in this next act—Act Four—
PLAYWRIGHT: which is actually the most important of all the
   acts in a melodrama.
BJJ: Act Four is the act which usually follows the Act Three
   "Climax," which you just saw.
PLAYWRIGHT: The fourth act sort of makes or breaks a show.
BJJ: It's sort of the spine of the whole drama—

PLAYWRIGHT: the hinge around which everything turns—

BJJ: not just in terms of the narrative but also just in terms of the sheer "theater" of a piece. You have a lot of stuff to do and it's really hard.

PLAYWRIGHT: Not only do you have to get the A plot—

BJJ: in this case, the story of Zoe and the estate—

PLAYWRIGHT: to intersect with B plot—

BJJ: in this case, the murder of Paul—

PLAYWRIGHT: but it's your last chance to really hit the audience with something big—

BJJ: like your best "theater trick," if you will.

PLAYWRIGHT: You have to push everything—actors, props, set, lights—to the limit somehow.

BJJ: They used to call it the "Sensation Scene"—

PLAYWRIGHT: because the idea is to overwhelm your audience's senses to the end of building the truest illusion of reality—

BJJ: regardless of whether or not it has anything to do with the plot.

PLAYWRIGHT: You're just supposed to make people think, for just a second, that what they're seeing is real and dangerous and sort of novel.

BJJ: Oh, and also, more often than not, Act Four is where the like moral of the play lives—

PLAYWRIGHT: Which is why I needed more white guys—

BJJ: because we're going to talk about universal themes—

PLAYWRIGHT (Brandishing the gavel): Like justice!

BJJ: and not "social issues."

PLAYWRIGHT: You basically sort of give your audience the moral, then you overwhelm them with fake destruction.

BJJ: Or something. It's just so hard. So I'm just going to tell you what happens, so we can keep going. I hope that's okay.

PLAYWRIGHT: Basically, it's later that night, and we're at the wharf, where we find Captain Ratts and his people like loading up the ship.

BJJ: A bunch of other white guys are there—

PLAYWRIGHT: Including George and Pete, who've just dropped off their last load of cotton ever, I guess, and then M'Closky enters and he's like, for no reason, except for exposition and maybe to be an asshole:

M'CLOSKY: You've got too much cotton on board—it can barely stay above the water level—and there's a small freight of turpentine in the forehold there, and one of the barrels leaks; a spark from your engines might set the ship on fire, and you'll go with it.

PLAYWRIGHT: Then suddenly there's all this commotion!

BJJ: And everyone's all:

PLAYWRIGHT: "What's going on?"

BJJ: And somebody's like:

PLAYWRIGHT: "We found the injiun! We found Wahnotee, the murderer! Let's lynch him for killing that little nigger boy who used to sing for us!"

BJJ: And Wahnotee lumbers on, being chased by a bunch of people, and everyone's about to like jump on him and fuck him up—

PLAYWRIGHT: but George is all:

GEORGE: Hold on! No violence—the critter don't know what we mean!

PLAYWRIGHT: But M'Closky, the real murderer, is all:

M'CLOSKY: Let him answer for the boy then. Down with him— lynch him! And the crowd's like:

(No one says anything for a second. BJJ and Playwright look at Assistant expectantly.)

ASSISTANT: "Lynch him!"

PLAYWRIGHT: And George's like:

GEORGE: Stan' back, I say! I'll nip the first that lays a finger on him—

BJJ: And they're basically all like:

PLAYWRIGHT: "But he killed the little slave boy who used to sing and dance for us!" And George's like:

GEORGE: I just don't think he killed Paul! It doesn't make any sense!

BJJ: And then someone's like:

PLAYWRIGHT: "Well we think he did kill him, so let's give him a trial like right now, since we've all got like fifteen minutes before we have to go."

BJJ: And someone's like:

ASSISTANT: "Who will be the accuser?"

BJJ: And everyone's like:

ASSISTANT: "M'Closky!"

M'CLOSKY: Wait, why me?

ASSISTANT: And they're like:

PLAYWRIGHT: "Because you were the one who was just shouting to lynch him—"

M'CLOSKY: Fine. I know then that the boy was killed with that tomahawk—the redskin owns it—the signs of violence are all 'round the shed—ain't it clear that in a drunken fit he slew the boy, and concealed the body yonder?

PLAYWRIGHT: And the crowd's all:

ASSISTANT: "Yeah! Yeah!"

And then someone is like:

PLAYWRIGHT: "Who will defend the indian?!"

ASSISTANT: And George's like:

GEORGE: I will; for it is against my nature to believe him guilty. And if he be, this isn't the place, nor you the authority to try him. I appeal against your usurped authority; this lynch law is a wild and lawless proceeding. You call yourselves judges—you aren't—you're a jury of executioners! Yonder, a poor, ignorant savage, and 'round him a circle of hearts, white with hate, thirsting for his blood. It is such scenes as these that bring disgrace upon our Western life.

M'CLOSKY: Evidence! Give us evidence! We've had talk enough; now for proof.

GEORGE: The proof is here, in my heart.

PETE: Stop, sar! Oh, laws-a-mussey—

BJJ: Oh right, also, like, randomly someone has brought on the camera that Wahnotee smashed after he found Paul dead—

PLAYWRIGHT: The same camera M'Closky stood in front of reading that letter—

BJJ: And randomly, I guess, George never looked in the camera or forgot about the camera? This is actually a hole in Boucicault's plot. Not mine.

PLAYWRIGHT: Anyway, Pete's like:

PETE: See dis! Here's a pictur' I found stickin' in that yar telescope machine, sar! Look, sar!

GEORGE: A photographic plate. What's this, eh? Two forms! The child—'tis he! Dead—and above him— Ah! ah! Jacob M'Closky, 'twas you murdered that—

(*Breaking character, becoming BJJ*) Wait, hold on, can we actually . . .

(*Assistant nods and exits.*)

PLAYWRIGHT: You know, it's really hard to describe how this scene works—

BJJ: Because it actually would have been really exciting one hundred and fifty years ago—having someone caught by a photograph.

PLAYWRIGHT: They were a very novel thing—

BJJ: Which is why this whole plot is more or less centered around a camera. But photographs to us? Boring. It's a cliché, but we've gotten so used to photos and photographic images that we basically do nothing but fake them, crop them, filter them, Photoshop them, so the kind of justice around which this whole thing hangs it's actually a little dated—

PLAYWRIGHT: But part of the thrill, part of the "Sensation" of the scene, was giving people back then a sense of having really witnessed something new and novel.

BJJ: And that's basically impossible for us to do now. If anything, the theater is no longer a place of novelty. The fact is we can more or less experience anything nowadays. So I think the final frontier, awkwardly enough, is probably just an actual experience of finality, I think.

PLAYWRIGHT: Like—death, basically?

BJJ: So for a while I was thinking maybe I could actually just set this place on fire with you inside—

PLAYWRIGHT: Bring you as close to death as possible . . . That would be amazing . . .

BJJ: And then, of course, rescue each of you one by one—

PLAYWRIGHT: And then perform the rest of the show out on the street.

BJJ: But that would be crazy.

PLAYWRIGHT: And also I would only be able to do this show once.

BJJ: I thought about actually just sacrificing an animal onstage—

PLAYWRIGHT: Like in the good old days—a goat or something—

BJJ: But, there are laws against that—

PLAYWRIGHT: And you don't have a petting zoo—

BJJ: Anyway, I figured I'd try something. I hope it isn't too disappointing.

(Assistant has wheeled out an overhead projector. He projects a lynching photograph on to the back wall. They perform the following in the light of the projection.)

Where was—okay, sorry, I lost my place. I'm going to go back:

GEORGE: I will; for it is against my nature to believe him guilty. And if he be, this isn't the place, nor you the authority to try him. I appeal against your usurped authority; this lynch law is a wild and lawless proceeding. You call yourselves judges—you aren't—you're a jury of executioners! Yonder, a poor, ignorant savage, and 'round him a circle of hearts, white with hate, thirsting for his blood. It is such scenes as these that bring disgrace upon our Western life.

M'CLOSKY: Evidence! Give us evidence. We've had talk enough; now for proof.

GEORGE: The proof is here, in my heart.

PETE: Stop, sar! Oh, laws-a-mussey, see dis! Here's a picture I found stickin' in that yar telescope machine, sar! Look, sar!

BJJ: I can't see anything. I'm sorry— Can we turn this off?

(The picture disappears.)

GEORGE: A photographic plate. What's this, eh? Two forms! The child—'tis he! Dead—and above him— Ah! ah! Jacob M'Closky, 'twas you murdered that boy!

M'CLOSKY: Me?

GEORGE: You! You slew him with that tomahawk; and as you stood over his body with the letter in your hand, you thought that no witness saw the deed, that no eye was on you—but there was, Jacob M'Closky, there was. The eye of the Eternal was on you—the blessed sun in Heaven, that, looking down, struck upon this plate the image of the deed.

M'CLOSKY: 'Tis false!

GEORGE: 'Tis true! The apparatus can't lie. Look there, jurymen. Oh, you wanted evidence—you called for proof—Heaven has answered and convicted you. You wanted to make us murder that injiun; but since we've got our hands in for justice, we'll try it on you. Shall we have one law for the redskin and another for the white? Jacob, your accuser is that picture of the crime—let that speak—defend yourself.

PLAYWRIGHT: And M'Closky pulls out a knife.

M'CLOSKY: I will, quicker than lightning!

PLAYWRIGHT: And someone is like: "Seize him!" And all these men rush on M'Closky and take away his knife and then George is like:

GEORGE: Stop! Search him—we may find more evidence.

ASSISTANT: "Here's a letter!"

GEORGE *(Opening the letter)*: What's here? "To Mrs. Peyton." Hello! I've got a hold of the tail of a rat. *(Reads)* What's this? A draft for eighty-five thousand dollars, and credit for the balance? You killed the boy to steal this letter from the mailbags—that the money should not arrive in time; had it done so, the lien on the estate would have ceased, and Zoe be free.

ASSISTANT: And everyone's like:

(Everyone includes everyone on and offstage.)

EVERYONE *(Loud, harsh, clear whisper)*: "Lynch him!"
GEORGE: Silence in the court. Stand back, let the gentlemen of the jury consult and return their verdict.
PETE *(Showing Wahnotee the photo)*: See, Injiun; look dar— You'se innocent—dar's de murderer of poor Paul.
WAHNOTEE: Ugh!
PETE: Closky tue Paul—kill de child with your, tomahawk dar. 'Twasn't you, no—poor injiun lub our little Paul.

(Wahnotee rises and looks at M'Closky.)

GEORGE: What say ye, gentlemen? Is the prisoner guilty, or is he not guilty?
ASSISTANT: And everyone's like:
EVERYONE *(Loud, harsh, clear whisper)*: "Guilty! Lynch him!"
GEORGE: And what is to be his punishment?
EVERYONE *(Loud, harsh, clear whisper)*: "Death! Lynch him!"
WAHNOTEE *(Crossing to M'Closky)*: Ugh!
PETE: You're a dead man, Mas'r Clusky—you got to believe dat.
M'CLOSKY: No-no! You are a white man; you'll not leave one of your own blood to be butchered by the redskin? If I must die for what I have done, give me up to the law; but save me from the tomahawk. Let me be tried!
GEORGE: You have been tried—and convicted. Providence has chosen your executioner. I shan't interfere.

PETE: O, no, Mas'r George, don't leave Mas'r Closky like dat—
'tain't what a good Christian should do.

GEORGE: D'ye hear that, Jacob? This old nigger—the grandfather of the boy you murdered—speaks for you—don't
that go through you?

WAHNOTEE *(His hand on M'Closky's skull)*: Wahnotee!

GEORGE *(Stopping Wahnotee)*: Whoa! No, Injiun, we deal justice here, not revenge; 'tisn't you he has injured, 'tis the
white man, whose laws he has offended.

PLAYWRIGHT: So Captain Ratts tells Pete and some men to
put M'Closky into the hold or hatch to await, I guess, his
hanging or whatever, and they take him down into the
hatch or the hold or whatever it's called and everyone's
like: "Well that's over," and go back to business as usual . . .

(Beat.)

But then, like thirty seconds later, Pete comes running up
being like:

(Assistant/Pete comes running back in.)

PETE: O, lawd, dat debil Closky, he tore hisself from de gent'lam,
knock me down, take my light, and trows it on de turpentine barrels, and now de cabin's all afire!

*(Fire sounds. The sound of men panicking. Actual fire would
be great. Pete exits.)*

PLAYWRIGHT: And basically the entire boat is on fire! And you sort
of see the flames engulfing everything—all the cotton—
everything!

ASSISTANT: There's general chaos—men running around, panicking, exiting the boat—an alarm starts ringing—and
then M'Closky:

M'CLOSKY: Ha! Burn! Burn! That's right. You thought you had cornered me, did ye? And now the road to escape is clear before me—and thus to secure it!

WAHNOTEE *(Appearing, raising his tomahawk)*: Paul.

M'CLOSKY: Devil!—you still here?! *(Pulls out his knife)* Stand clear!

(Wahnotee strikes the knife out of M'Closky's hand with his tomahawk, and then M'Closky starts to back away, but Wahnotee throws off his blanket and strikes at M'Closky several times. M'Closky avoids Wahnotee before Wahnotee catches his arm, and they struggle violently for the tomahawk, but Wahnotee wins, obviously, and drags him along the ground, taking up M'Closky's knife and repeatedly stabbing him with it, until M'Closky is bloody and nearly dead, but still screaming. It seems incredibly real.

And then Wahnotee finds some rope, wraps it around M'Closky's neck, starts dragging him off.)

(Choking) SOMEBODY!
HELP! HELP! HELP! HELP! HELP! HELP! HELP!
HELP! HELP! HELP! HELP! HELP! HELP! HELP!

(They exit as the noise and the flames build and build and build and build before, suddenly, lights and sound cut out completely, everything plunged in darkness and quiet. Assistant wanders in carrying a small flame or lantern.)

ASSISTANT/PETE *(In the darkness)*: Then the boat explodes.

(Cotton rains down on the audience. Or not.
Sensation.
Beat.)

Anyway. The whole point of this thing was to make you feel something. What does that mean? I have no idea, but I came here to tell you a story.

(Assistant/Pete exits.)

FIVE

Outside the sole-lit cabin in the abandoned negroes' quarters. It is night.

Zoe is discovered.

ZOE: It wants some hours yet to daylight and soon that man—
M'Closky—my master, will come for me: He has paid my
price, and he only consented to let me remain here this one
night, because Mrs. Peyton promised to give me up to him
today. Where is the negroes' quarters? Ah, yes. Here they
are. *(Knocks)* They are abandoned but—no, I see a light.

DIDO *(Entering from cabin)*: Who dat?

ZOE: Mammy! 'Tis I—Zoe.

DIDO *(Taken aback by her word choice, then)*: Missy Zoe! Why
are you out in de swamp dis time ob night? And you is all
wet! Missy Zoe, you catch de fever for sure!

ZOE: Auntie, that is why I've come. There is already sickness
up at the house: I have been up all night beside one who
suffers, and, Mammy, you are wise—you know every

plant, don't you, and what it is good for? I remembered that when I had the fever you gave me a drink, a bitter drink that made me sleep—do you remember it?

DIDO: Dat drink is fust-rate for de fever. Is de folks' head bad?

ZOE: Very bad, Mammy; and the heart aches worse, so they can get no rest.

DIDO: Hold on a bit, I get you a bottle.

(Dido exits into the cabin. Zoe is alone for a bit. An owl hoots. Dido reenters with a bottle.)

Here 'tis—now you give one timbleful—dat's nuff.

ZOE: All there is there would kill one, wouldn't it?

DIDO: Guess it could kill a dozen.

ZOE: It's not a painful death, Mammy, is it? You told me it produced a long, long sleep.

DIDO: Why you speak so wild? What you's gwine to do, missy? Why you tremble so?

ZOE: Give it to me.

DIDO: No. You want to hurt yourself! O, Zoe, why you ask Dido for dis pizin?

ZOE: Listen to me. I love one who is here, and he loves me— George. I sat outside his door all night and heard his sighs—his agony—torn from him by my coming fate; and he said, "I'd rather see her dead than his!"

DIDO: Dead!

ZOE: He said so before he left for the landing with Pete. I cried for hours before I rose up with the resolve to end my own life! For his sake! I stole from the house, and ran down to the bayou; but its cold, black stream terrified me—drowning must be so horrible a death. I could not do it. Then, as I knelt there, weeping for courage, a snake rattled beside me. I shrunk from it and fled. Death was right there next me, and I dared not take it. O! I'm afraid to die; yet I am more afraid to live.

DIDO: Die!

ZOE: So I came here to you; to you, my own dear mammy, who so often hushed me to sleep when I was a child. You can protect me from the man—do let me die without pain, that I may never leave my home—my dear, dear home.

DIDO: No, no—

ZOE: O! Good, good nurse: You will not give me to that man? Your own Zoe, that loves you, Mammy, so much. *(Gets bottle away from Dido)* Ah! I have it.

DIDO: No, missy. O! No—don't!

ZOE: Hush!

(Zoe runs off. Dido looks off after her. Minnie comes to the door, holding a jug of something. She's a little tipsy.)

MINNIE: Girl, who was that?

DIDO: Zoe. That bitch just ran off wit all your medicine—I think she about to poison herself!

MINNIE: What? Why?

DIDO: Cuz she is in love wit that white man.

MINNIE *(Shaking her head)*: Hmhmhm. Zoe is such a mess.

(They both look off after Zoe for a beat. Dido is clearly upset about something. It takes a moment to surface.)

DIDO: And you know she kept calling me Mammy! And I was like, "Bitch, what? We are basically the same age!"

MINNIE: Whaaat?

DIDO: I can't believe that shit. Do I look that old to you?

MINNIE: No, girl. Black don't crack. That bitch is just crazy. That's what happens when you hang out wit all these damn white people all the damn time. Let it go.

DIDO: Naw, Minnie! Shit!

MINNIE: Come on, girl! Stop freaking out. She ain't worth it. We 'bout to be livin' on a boat and here you are letting these light-skinned haters get you down. Come on, help me finish packing.

(Beat.)

DIDO *(Collecting herself)*: You right. Moving just always be stressin' me out.

MINNIE: I know, right?

DIDO: Heifer, how would you know? You been on this plantation yo' whole life!

MINNIE: Oh, right.

(Beat.)

DIDO *(Sucks her teeth)*: And how are you just now starting to pack when we leaving in like an hour?

MINNIE: I ain't know it took this long. I ain't neva had to move before, girl.

DIDO: It's wrapping up all yo' damn voodoo dolls that's taking so damn long.

MINNIE *(Hurt)*: Don't talk about my collectibles like that . . .

(Beat.)

Why are you freakin' out at me like this? I thought we wuz girls?

(Beat.)

DIDO *(Collecting herself)*: I'm sorry, Minnie. I just don't like when people be treating me like I'm some old woman. I am not a mammy! I'm not!

MINNIE *(Realizes why Dido is upset, then)*: It's okay, girl. I forgive you. *(Embraces Dido)* But we gotta be good to one anutha. You know all we got is each other now.

DIDO: You right.

(They un-embrace.)

You think we should go tell somebody?

MINNIE: Tell somebody what?

DIDO: That Zoe is 'bout to poison herself.

MINNIE: Who you gonna tell?

DIDO: I don't know. Mrs. Peyton?

MINNIE: Girl, stop. These people ain't our problem anymore. We 'bout to be livin' on a boat!

(She looks at Dido, who seems unexcited.)

I'm worried about you.

DIDO: Why?

MINNIE: I think you can get too worked up over small stuff. Stop being so sensitive and caring so much about other people and what they think about you or you gonna catch yourself a stroke, for real. You can't be bringing your work home with you. If Zoe's light-skinned ass wanna call you old and go poison herself over some white man, then you need to let her do that and move on. She's an adult. You can't change her. Shit. Same thing with Mrs. Peyton. And Miss Dora. And Massa George. And Massa M'Closky. I know we slaves and evurthang, but you are not your job. You gotta take time out of your day to live life for you.

(Dido starts crying, softly.)

Oh, girl! What's wrong?

DIDO: I just don't know what I'm supposed to be doing better.

MINNIE: What?

DIDO: To be happy. I don't like feeling the way I do. This life— I didn't ask for it.

MINNIE: Didn't nobody ask for they lives, girl.

DIDO: I know. I just don't know what I'm supposed to do with that.

(Minnie comforts her.)

MINNIE: Well, listen: I'll tell you what you need to do right now. You need to come back inside, help me finish packing, have one more drink, get a little catnap, put on your nice slave tunic, and get ready for your life to change. We 'bout to be on a boat, and it may not be Heaven, but it's sho' as hell different than this here swamp, and that's got to mean something. Plus, I'm getting cold standing out here.

DIDO: Yeah, let's go back inside.

(They start to head back in.)

MINNIE: You know, I would be so pissed if something were to happen that somehow rendered these last twelve hours totally moot.

DIDO: I know, right? I was thinking the same thing. Like if these white folks found out like . . . Massa Closky like . . . killed Paul or something to intercept the letter that was supposed to save the plantation.

MINNIE: Wait— There was a letter that was supposed to save the plantation?

DIDO: Yes, girl. Haven't you heard Zoe and Mrs. Peyton going on and on about it? Every breakfast they been talking about it.

MINNIE: They do?

DIDO: Yes, girl. Where is your mind?

MINNIE: I must have zoned out. You know I be getting so bored.

DIDO: Girl, you are such a trip. Anyway, finish telling me about that rabbit.

(Minnie and Dido exit. The little light there slowly starts to fade. Meanwhile, there are night sounds: crickets chirping, an owl's hoot. And, right before it gets too dark to see, Br'er Rabbit wanders in with a gavel and a tomahawk. As the lights fully die, he looks right as us. Then a blackout, in which there is singing. Everyone sings.)

END OF PLAY

BRANDEN JACOBS-JENKINS's plays include *Everybody* (Signature Theatre, Pulitzer Prize finalist), *War* (LCT3/Lincoln Center Theater), *Gloria* (Vineyard Theatre, Pulitzer Prize finalist), *Appropriate* (Signature Theatre, Obie Award), *An Octoroon* (Soho Rep., Obie Award) and *Neighbors* (The Public Theater). He is a Residency Five playwright at Signature Theatre and under commission from LCT3/Lincoln Center Theater, the Manhattan Theatre Club/Sloan Initiative Grant, and the Steppenwolf Theatre Company. His recent honors include the Charles Wintour Award for Promising Playwright from the *London Evening Standard*, a London Critics Circle Award for Most Promising Playwright, a MacArthur Fellowship, the Windham-Campbell Prize for Drama, the Benjamin H. Danks Award from the American Academy of Arts and Letters, the PEN/Laura Pels International Foundation Theater Award, the Steinberg Playwright Award, and the inaugural Tennessee Williams Award. He sits on the board of Soho Rep., and, with Annie Baker, is the Associate Co-Director of the Hunter College MFA Program in Playwriting, where he is also a Master-Artist-in-Residence.

Theatre Communications Group would like to offer our special thanks to the Vilcek Foundation for its generous support of the publication of Appropriate/An Octoroon: Plays *by Branden Jacobs-Jenkins*

THE VILCEK FOUNDATION raises awareness of immigrant contributions in America and fosters appreciation of the arts and sciences. Established in 2000 by Jan and Marica Vilcek, immigrants from the former Czechoslovakia, the Foundation's mission was inspired by the couple's respective careers in biomedical science and art history, as well as their appreciation for the opportunities offered to them as newcomers to the United States. TCG books sponsored by the Vilcek Foundation include:

Appropriate/An Octoroon: Plays, Branden Jacobs-Jenkins
Cost of Living, Martyna Majok
The Detroit Project, Dominique Morisseau
Five Plays, Sam Hunter
Miss You Like Hell, Quiara Alegría Hudes and Erin McKeown
Mr. Burns and Other Plays, Anne Washburn

THEATRE COMMUNICATIONS GROUP (TCG), the national organization for the American theatre, promotes the idea of "A Better World for Theatre, and a Better World Because of Theatre." In addition to TCG's numerous services to the theatre field, TCG Books is the nation's largest independent publisher of dramatic literature, with 16 Pulitzer Prizes for Drama on its book list. The book program commits to the life-long career of its playwrights, keeping all of their plays in print. TCG Books' other authors include: Annie Baker, Nilo Cruz, Athol Fugard, David Henry Hwang, Tony Kushner, Donald Margulies, Lynn Nottage, Suzan-Lori Parks, Sarah Ruhl, Stephen Sondheim, Anne Washburn, and August Wilson, among many others.

Support TCG's work in the theatre field by becoming a member or donor: www.tcg.org

tcg